RAJA YOGA
new beginnings

Compiled and written by Ken O'Donnell

Recommended reading
for Raja Yoga students
who have completed
the introductory course

new beginnings by Ken O'Donnell
© Copyright 2021 Brahma Kumaris Australia

Published by EternityInk
181 First Avenue, Five Dock NSW 2046
Email: info@eternityink.com.au

ISBN 978-0-9587230-8-4

First printing 1987
Second printing 1988
Third printing 1989
Fourth printing 1993
Fifth printing 1996
Sixth printing 2000
Seventh printing 2004
Eighth printing 2021

This book has been produced by the Brahma Kumaris World Spiritual University, a non-profit organisation, with the aim of sharing information as a service for the spiritual growth of individuals. There are Brahma Kumaris Centres in over 70 countries worldwide.

No part of this publication may be reproduced, stored in a retrieval system, or transmitted, in any form or by any means, manual, electronic, mechanical, photocopying, recording, or otherwise without the prior written permission of the copyright owner.
All rights reserved.

Contents

Preface		4
Foreword		7
Chapter 1	The Soul	9
Chapter 2	Soul Consciousness – The Gateway to God	23
Chapter 3	God	37
Chapter 4	Karma and Yoga	50
Chapter 5	Raja Yoga and the Wheel of Life	65
Chapter 6	The Human World Tree	92
Chapter 7	The Essence of Raja Yoga	108
Chapter 8	Perfection – The Transformation of the Self	126
Chapter 9	Advanced Stages of Raja Yoga	143
Chapter 10	The Spiritual Revolution	152

Preface

As the world plunges deeper and deeper into one crisis after another, an ever-growing number of people are witnessing the rebirth of all that is true and noble in the human heart: on one side, the clamour for change, liberation, independence and equality; and on the other, the perception that the change required is not simply a matter of economics or politics but one that touches the core of our natures, attitudes and visions.

On seeing the almost complete rupture of human values, the mad rush towards an 'apocalypse', many have retired into their own cells of desperation with the feeling of abandonment. 'Even God has left us!' they cry, yet the throes of death have always signalled new beginnings . . .

This book is a story of the rekindling of the soul and how, through the opening of the eye of wisdom, one can see a brilliant future rising like a phoenix from the ashes of waste and corruption of this old world. It is a simple, step-by-step guide for those who recognise that now is the time for the rising up of the individual from the mire of its own weaknesses, the time for actively making the only valid contribution to a new and elevated world order – the transformation of the self.

This book is about the original and ancient system of yoga – *Raja Yoga*. *Yoga* generally has the connotation of some physical or breathing exercises, but its deepest definition is 'the mental union or link between the individual soul and the Supreme Being, or God'.

Raja means *king*, so *Raja Yoga* can be understood in various ways:
- the King of Yogas or the Royal Yoga;
- the yoga through which the soul becomes a sovereign over its mind, intellect and personality, thereby ruling the sense organs of the body and being in complete control of any situation.

Raja Yoga was first taught 5,000 years ago in India but, in the course of time, the original spiritual methods and principles which kept souls in communion with the Supreme Soul were overlaid by other practices, and the aim of complete perfection of the human being was put aside as untenable. Recently, however, those original methods of how to contact the Supreme Soul through thoughts (meditation) have been revealed again, making the spiritual endeavour towards complete self-transformation easy and natural. To make the meditation more meaningful a whole series of introductions are offered: who we are, where we are from, where we're going, who God is, what His role is and how to develop a relationship with Him so that peace, love, wisdom and bliss flow into the soul, restoring it to its rightful authority over matter. Understanding all these points helps us to stabilise ourselves in such a state of self-confidence that not only does our own life take on a completely new and marvellous hue, but we find ourselves able to inspire many others to take up the challenge of creating a new world of self-change.

In India, the Brahma Kumaris World Spiritual University was set up in 1937 to study and practise the teachings of Raja Yoga, and to make them available to all humanity regardless of colour, sex, age, creed or caste. I first made contact with this organisation in London in 1975 while on a tour of personal investigation of the world's major faiths.

That journey, through many countries and myriad experiences, has led me to the conclusion that the human dilemma has no cultural boundaries; that greed, arrogance, frustration, anger and violence have no nationality, race or sex, no preference for rich or poor, old or young. While we may live on different decks, we are all 'in the same boat' and whether sunning ourselves on the first-class deck or sweating it out in the boiler-room, humanity's boat has one course. At the moment it appears that we are aboard a rudderless craft proceeding aimlessly. In the midst of my own internal complications, I was sure there existed a unity of principle behind the masks of humanity. But as I saw the grotesqueness of the world around and my own inadequacy at dealing with it, the birth of self-respect in the soul was unimaginable.

It was in this consciousness that I entered the Spiritual University's London branch and received my first injection of optimism. Immediately I sensed there was something different here. Whether it was the complete simplicity and absence of ritualistic forms, or the purity that the sisters radiated while greeting or explaining what Raja Yoga was, or the clear and logical terms that they used, from the first I felt that I had arrived 'home'.

Taking daily instruction for some months and entering into the rhythm of yogic life, I found the ignorance that I had perpetuated in myself, during so many years, melting away in the face of concise and logical explanations of everything that I had always wanted to know, and even more. There was the experience of breaking out of a shell like a bird when it is born. Until the moment of birth, the bird thinks that the only world that exists is the one within the shell. Then it cracks the shell and emerges, discovering the vastness of the world outside. When absorbing this knowledge, the vision of the world I had had also 'cracked' and my eyes opened to the wonder of the eternal laws that govern everything. The world inside the shell just appeared so limited and didn't seem real anymore. Internally there was the experience of greater and greater self-control, and I could see the result of my self-change in the mirror of others and the reactions in which I found myself. With these initial proofs came the natural inspiration to make efforts to achieve the lofty goal of complete self-transformation.

The same knowledge, from which so many souls have derived so much benefit, is set out in this book. Though containing the basic points of the introductory course given by the Spiritual University, an attempt has been made to relate everything to meditation, while at the same time maintaining simple and concise language and steering away from a theoretical stance. Therefore, the knowledge is explained as much as possible from the experiential point of view, interspersed with poetry and meditation exercises.

Om Shanti

Om Shanti are two Sanskrit words which mean *'I, the soul, exist in a state of peace.'* The state of peace, which everyone is searching for, is evoked in our awareness by these words. They remind us that the qualities that give us life belong to the soul and not to the body.

Acknowledgements

Multimillion thanks to beloved Bapdada, Dadiji, Didiji, Dadi Jankiji and all the dear sisters and brothers whose classes, articles and comments form the basis of the material in this book.

Ken O'Donnell

Foreword

What then the toys of men?
Something is missing.
We've classified and categorised,
Labels and fables.
We move faster than the lions,
Cut through the skies above,
Dive so deeply in the ocean,
But we've forgotten how to love.
What then the dreams of men?
Something is missing.
Planning and negotiating,
Breaking ideals.
We have built the tallest buildings,
Sent out missions to the stars,
Everyone tries to be a success,
But we've forgotten who we are.
What then the works of men?
Something is missing.
Building up and breaking down,
Sorrows and ambitions.
We created all the boundaries,
Yet we wonder where peace has gone,
We cannot see the destination,
We've forgotten where we're from.
What then the words of men?
Something is missing.
Ancient volumes and sacred texts,
Mountains of information.
What then the lives of men?
It's the love-link that's missing.
The bridges had been breached,
And no one was crossing.
Sure we'd crawled across our history,
Scrambling orphans in the dust,
Tired and trembling and broken down,
We'd forgotten Who to trust.

Editor's note

In Raja Yoga, although God, the Supreme Soul, is referred to by the male pronoun He, *it should be understood that God is neither male nor female but a soul, a being without any physical form. To help develop a sense of close relationship with God a personal pronoun is often used. In Raja Yoga it is experienced that God is a personal being with whom we can truly have the relationship of both father and mother.*

Chapter 1 The Soul

Introduction

The world is full of many wonders, incredible works of art and architecture, of science and invention – but the greatest of them all by far is the human mind. It is the mind's play that brings about all activity in the human world. The outline of everything people construct is first formed in the mind and then filled in with matter to assume a concrete shape. History, science, culture, trade and commerce – in fact, all knowledge and systems of our day-to-day world are but the projection and fulfilment of thoughts. If, by concentrating itself on matter, the mind can work such wonders and help us attain such miraculous physical powers as we have, what can it not attain if it concentrates on itself?

Disorder and tension on the individual level and, consequently, on the social level are the result of ignorance of the self and the world around, such that the mind stays without rest. It runs, jumps and churns aimlessly, lashed by waves of feelings and emotions. Like a spider caught in its own web, the individual becomes entangled in nets which are the consequences of this ignorance of the fundamentals of life.

In this chapter we begin an upward journey that will take the reader through deeper and deeper levels of understanding and experience, which create freedom from these nets.

This chapter deals with:
- The distinction between soul and matter – the metaphysical and the physical.
- The anatomy of the human soul.
- The process of experiencing or bringing out higher emotions.

The distinction between the soul and matter

In life many happenings cannot be explained solely in material terms. At certain points of crisis or inspiration, there are deep emotional and spiritual experiences which separate us from the world around. We retreat at such times: into ourselves, into religious or philosophical books;

perform rituals or adopt symbols, in order to understand these experiences. We are subject to a perpetual commentary on life from our own thoughts, feelings and deductions.

These faculties of thinking and forming ideas, desiring and deciding, (and all the different aspects which constitute our individual personality) are non-physical, and yet real. Indeed, anything perceptible to us comes from two sources: what is detected by the physical senses and what arises from impressions recorded on these subtle faculties. The things that we can see, taste, hear, smell and feel, as well as the body itself, are formed of matter. But the subtle faculties of mind, intellect and personality are manifest in what is called consciousness.

Consciousness is another word for *soul* or *spirit*. The soul is a subtle entity that cannot be measured by any physical process or instrumentation. The non-material part of each one of us exists and is in fact the true self, or what we simply call *I*. This *I*, or soul, is perceptible only at the level of mind and intellect.

The soul must first be aware of its own powers to perceive, discriminate and understand, in order to attune these powers to the proper degree of subtlety and precision. With the physical eyes we can see only gross, material things. It requires a different kind of vision or outlook to 'see' that which concerns the non-material, all those experiences which transcend this physical level of existence. Raja Yoga involves the development and refinement of the so-called *third eye* so that we not only 'see' spiritually but understand and adjust to what we 'see' in the most natural way possible.

Atom and atma

Since the 17th century scientists have built up knowledge of the laws of the physical universe leading to the emergence of atomic theory. The atom is described as being a point source of energy, and different energy levels and vibrations between neighbouring atoms give the appearance of form, colour and heat. The English word *atom* came from the Latin *atomus* which means *the twinkling of an eye* and the Greek *atomos* meaning *indivisible*. The Greek word is similar to the Hindi *atma* which means *self* or *soul* and refers to the conscious energy of the human as being an indivisible and indestructible point of non-physical light.

It has been established that the entire material world we see around us as a variety of forms and colours, light and heat, is formed of these point – sources of physical energy. The most beautiful scene in nature is merely a pattern of energy waves and vibrations. The sense organs select the vibrations and relay a message to the mind where all images are formed. The eyes see some of these patterns as light forms and colours; the nose picks up odours. In the same way sounds, tastes and sensations are detected and transmitted to the mind.

The human body is also a complex pattern of physical energies. Atomic particles build together to form the organic structures and inorganic minerals which perform the body's chemical interactions, thus forming the basis of the hormonal and nervous control of the body. What we see as old or young, ugly or beautiful, male or female, is also the effect of these differing levels of physical energies. However marvellous a machine the body may be, it is the presence of the soul which makes it function. One of the basic differences between souls and atoms is that while souls can exercise choice of their movements, where and when to go somewhere, atoms cannot obviously exercise such choice. In a way you could say that a soul is a point-source of spiritual energy that has awareness of its own existence. Atoms do not.

Author's experience: detachment from the body

As I sat down, I tried to think of myself as a spiritual being, a point-source of conscient energy centred in the forehead. After some minutes I became aware that my attention was leaving the various limbs and organs of the body. It was as if there were a rush of energy rising slowly, like mercury in a thermometer, towards the area in the centre between the eyebrows. Then, very suddenly, I had the feeling that I was totally bodiless, without any weight or heaviness. There was a deep feeling of detachment from the physical surroundings. Even though l was acutely aware of the things around, I was seeing them completely in an observer state; I was just a tiny point of consciousness, surrounded by a lot of movement, forms, colours and sounds of which I was not part.

Soul, body and the *third eye*

Human being means the consciousness, the soul or *being*, experiencing life through the insentient body, the *human*. The body is perishable and temporary, whereas the soul is eternal and without physical dimension. The soul is the driver; the body is the car. The soul is the guest; the body is the hotel. The soul is the actor; the body is the costume. The soul is the musician; the body is the instrument. I can use a knife to cut a tomato. I can use the same knife to stab someone. The knife neither decides nor experiences, but can be washed easily under the tap.

Now look at the fingers which held the knife. They neither decide nor experience the actions. They too can be washed under the tap. It's easy to realise that the knife is an instrument, but it is more difficult to realise that the fingers are instruments too, and not only the fingers but the arms too. The legs are instruments for walking, the eyes for seeing, the ears for hearing, the mouth for speaking, breathing, tasting, the heart for pumping food and oxygen around the body, and so on. Even the brain is an instrument used like a computer to express all thought, word and action programmes through the body and to experience the results. If every physical part of the body is an instrument, who or what is it that is using the instrument?

Very simply it is *I*, the self, the soul. The soul uses the word *I* for itself and the word *my* when referring to the body: *my* hand, *my* mouth, *my* brain, etc. *I* am different from *my* body.

Where is the soul situated in the body?

The dualities of matter/anti-matter, sentient/insentient, physical/spiritual can be understood easily with the awareness of the mechanism by which human consciousness operates through the body. The soul has three basic functions to perform: to give and maintain life, to express and experience its role, and to receive the rewards or fruits of past actions performed in previous existences. *(See Chapter 4)*

These functions are controlled and monitored through the nervous and hormonal systems from a particular point in the area of the brain housing the thalamus, hypothalamus, pituitary and pineal glands. This region is known as the seat of the soul, or the *third eye*. The connection between the physical and the non-physical is by the medium of thought energy. Many religions, philosophies and esoteric studies place great importance on the *third eye*, or *eye of the mind*.

When viewed from the front, this region appears to be between and slightly above the line of the eyebrows. It's for this reason that Hindus use a *tilak,* a dot in red or sandalwood paste in the middle of the forehead. Christians also make the sign of the cross in this region. Even when one makes a mistake or expresses tiredness, it's to this region that we put the hands in the characteristic gestures of self-dismay or exhaustion. After all, the soul subconsciously knows that it makes the mistakes and not the body. When people are frowning or concentrating deeply in thought, it is this area of the forehead that creases into lines on the skin.

The form of the soul

In deep meditation one can perceive the soul as an infinitesimal point of non-physical light surrounded by an oval-shaped aura. The soul is not an invisible or ethereal duplicate of the physical body. The *soul energy* which manifests as thoughts and feelings has no physical size and for this simple reason it is eternal. Something which has no physical size cannot be destroyed.

The anatomy of the soul

When the soul is in the body, it manifests as three faculties. Although each faculty can be given a different name, it is actually the same energy, the soul, functioning on three different levels simultaneously. These are the mind, the intellect and the memories, or *sanskaras*.

Mind is the thinking faculty of the soul. It is the mind that imagines, thinks and forms ideas. The thought process is the basis of all emotions, desires and sensations. It is through this faculty that, in an instant, thoughts can be projected to a distant place, past experiences and emotions can be relived or even the future anticipated. It is the mind that experiences the variations of moods. The mind is a faculty of the soul, not to be confused with the heart or even the brain.

Intellect is used to assess thoughts. This is the faculty of understanding and decision-making which stands out as the most crucial faculty of the three. With the deepening and broadening of the intellect, clear understanding and realisation of knowledge becomes natural, and the power to decide and reason becomes clear. It is the intellect which remembers, discriminates, judges and exercises its power in the form of will.

Sanskaras is a Hindi word which best describes what we could call *impressions* or *subconscious or unconscious mind*. They are the record of all the soul's past experiences and actions. *Sanskaras* can take the forms of habits, talents, emotional temperaments, personality traits, beliefs, values or instincts. Every action as an experience either creates a *sanskar* (this is how a habit begins), or reinforces an old one. Whatever impression is etched in the soul remains within the soul, forming a complete archive of all the experiences that the soul has had. When we speak of defects, specialities or virtues, we are referring to the *sanskaras*. The *sanskaras* are the basis of the soul's individuality.

Origin of thought

The cyclic nature of the thought process is shown in the diagram on the opposite page. From the *sanskaras* various subconscious impressions surface in the conscious mind and manifest as thoughts, emotions or desires. These are then processed by the intellect and may be expressed as actions through the body. The way in which we act, the results of our actions and the input data from the external world, collected through the sense organs, all leave more impressions on the soul. These create or reinforce *sanskaras* or cancel the effect of others. If an action is performed repeatedly it becomes a deep *sanskara*, which will then be most likely to re-emerge in the consciousness in the future (ie as a habit). The great majority of observations and actions leave only a weak impression on the soul so that the soul is unable to recall exactly all that has taken place. Only stronger impressions form the basis of what is filed away as memories of the past.

Quality of thought

Some experiences have been positive and beneficial for the soul, while others have been harmful. Based on this classification, the quality of thought is judged. So I can ask myself: has a particular thought come from an 'impure' *sanskara*, a *sanskara* formed from an experience of disharmony or peacelessness? Will this thought bring further peacelessness to the soul? Will it create disharmony or sorrow in others? Or has this thought arisen from a positive and pure *sanskara*, which will create and maintain peace and harmony in the soul?

Choice of thought

Thought is the seed of action and experience. When there is the desire for pure experience, coupled with the realisation of the importance of the quality of thought, then naturally those seeds will be selected which will bear the desired fruit. The desire may be for peace, knowledge, contentment, love, power, joy, insight; any one of a number of positive experiences may be savoured. And, of course, there will then be the aim to control or eradicate those thoughts and *sanskaras* which are the seeds of disharmony and peacelessness. The mechanism by which the soul can select its desired thoughts and emotions is the intellect.

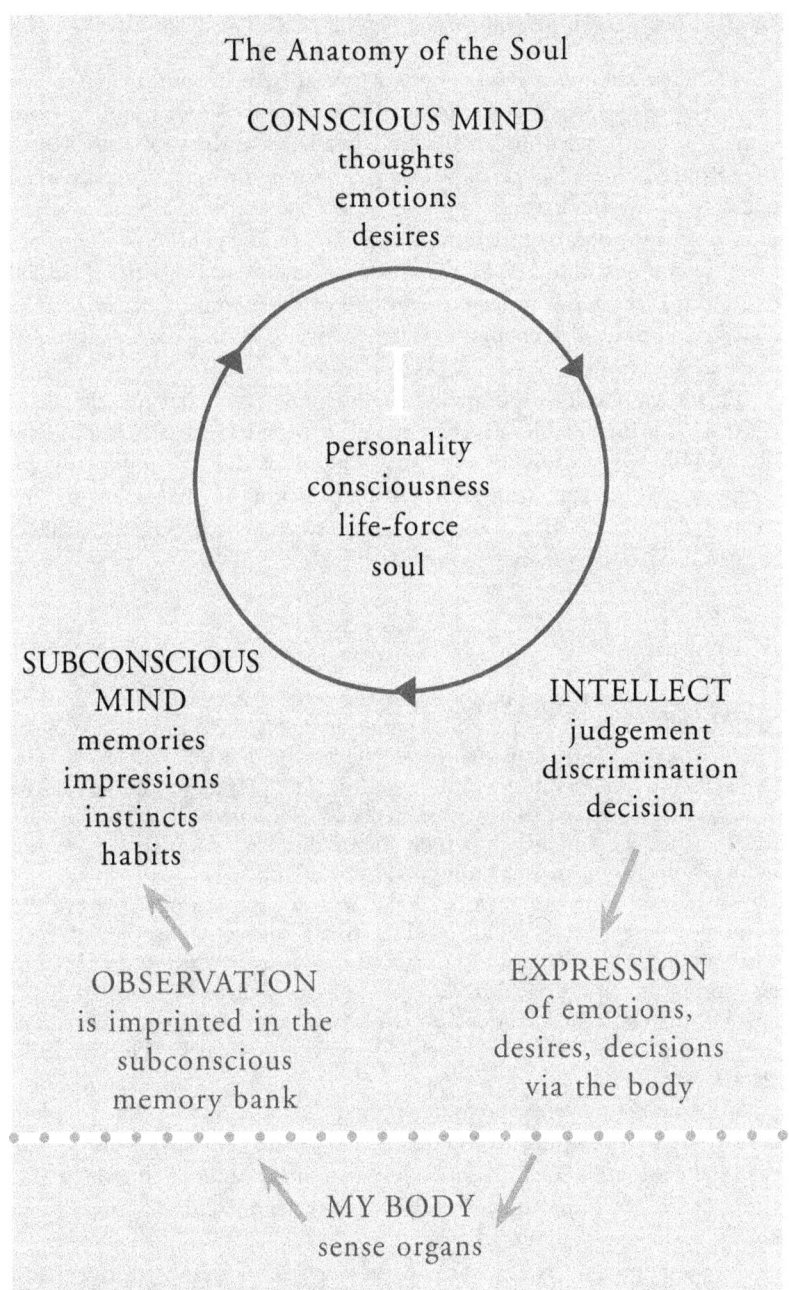

Intellect – 'will power'

The expression *will power* is often used to refer to our ability to put into practice the ideals we know to be for our well-being and to resist activity which is harmful. This is directly related to the soul's intellectual strength. When we speak of weakness or strength in the soul, we are referring to the intellect. In the case of a weak soul it is almost as if the intellect plays no part in determining which thoughts arise in the mind, but they come as if pushed by the *sanskaras* (mainly in the form of habits) or are triggered by the atmosphere around or the moods of others. On the contrary, a powerful soul enjoys the experience of its own choice regardless of external stimuli.

Raja Yoga develops the intellect to such an extent that this degree of control is feasible. A Raja Yogi can be in the midst of a situation of intense disturbance and yet remain so unshakeably calm that the inner strength becomes a solace and inspiration to others lacking in that strength. The weak soul is like a leaf at the mercy of the storm; the strong one is like a rock in the face of a tempestuous sea.

Mind-games

Let's see what is happening inside the soul. It is rather like a football game in which there are two sides and a field. The field in this case is the mind, but this is a field which 'feels' the movements of the players. The two sides are the *sanskaras* and the intellect. The players on the side of the *sanskaras* are habits, beliefs, memories, tendencies, instincts and personality traits, while the intellect has judgement, discrimination, the power of memory, decision, understanding, will-power and so on.

In the case of a weakened soul the *sanskaras* are stronger players and dominate the game, using all possible 'tricks' to overpower the intellect. The intellect's players are without power and don't really know how to play properly. Will-power is the goal-keeper. Will-power says to itself, 'Well, those habits and tendencies have scored so many "goals" in the past, just one more won't make much difference to the self. The *sanskaras* always win.'

If the *sanskaras* were a 'good' team then all would be fine. The problem is they are full of impurities and defects, and every time they 'score a goal' the intellect is weakened. Meanwhile, the mind is experiencing the whole game, with the emotions, feelings and thoughts coming and going according to the quality of the game.

Now, if the soul really wants to have peace of mind, it's not just a question of clearing it of all thoughts as done in some forms of meditation – that is, clearing the field of all players. No doubt because there is no game happening, there would be some tranquillity experienced; but, after the attention of keeping the mind free from thoughts is withdrawn, the same players who were there before will return without having been changed in any way. Similarly, if we clear the field and replace the players of the *sanskaras* and intellect by a *mantra* (incantation of some sacred syllables), candle flame or any other form of concentration, there will no doubt be the experience of tranquillity, but again as soon as the attention is withdrawn, the former players return without having been changed and the tensions that were there previously will also return.

In order to have lasting and unshakeable peace of mind or rather peace in the 'field' of the mind, instead of just a passing experience of tranquillity, it is necessary to change the players so that the game is one of perfect harmony. For this the intellect needs power and knowledge so that it can participate effectively in the game and the *sanskaras* need to be purified so that all defects and 'dirty' tricks are removed. For this reason the only type of meditation that brings real and permanent peace of mind is that which fills the intellect with strength and wisdom and brings purity to the *sanskaras*. When strength and wisdom unite, the result is peace. When the soul is aware of its true identity and is linked with the Supreme Soul, power surges into the soul through the intellect, purifying the *sanskaras* and bringing peace to the mind. Even after a few minutes some transformation in all the 'players' can be noticed and, when the soul concentrates on other tasks or faces other situations, they behave completely harmoniously. This type of meditation will be dealt with in more detail in Chapter 3.

The process of bringing out higher emotions

As has been mentioned already, Raja Yoga gives the intellect the power to select those positive *sanskaras* which lead to the higher emotions, calm and clear thoughts and the pure desire to enjoy life in such a way that no sorrow is experienced for the self and no sorrow is given to others. In the initial stages of meditation, the yogi calms the mind and experiences *sanskaras* which in most people surface only occasionally, as they are deeper than the superficial memories of worldly experiences. These are the pure and powerful *sanskaras* relating to the eternal nature of the soul. As the soul is not a material energy, but is a metaphysical energy separate from the body, then the dualities of the material world do not relate to the deep, inner nature of the soul. Consciousness has the same property as light, a powerful force with distinct qualities yet having no gravitational mass. In fact, the only 'pull' or 'burden' on the soul is the result of its own impure thoughts and negative actions.

So the Raja Yogi sees more deeply than these superficial *sanskaras* and sees the real nature of the soul: peace, purity, power and contentment. When these original *sanskaras* are experienced, then love and happiness are also experienced automatically. After some practice, the Raja Yogi has the intellectual power to bring these *sanskaras* out consciously into daily life at any time. In a situation which would lead most people to experience negative moods or emotions such as fear, depression, anxiety, boredom, fatigue, hatred or aggression, the Raja Yogi becomes detached and brings forth the inner powers of contentment and tranquillity. This of course is beneficial not only for the self but also for others.

Personal experience of the author

I used to think of peace as being intimately related to the beauty of nature – the play of waves on a beach, the rustle of wind through a forest, the soaring and swooping of gulls – in short, anything removed from the rush and bustle of the city. Alternatively, I would associate peace with some physical form of relaxation like headphones plugged into soothing music, a hot bath after a hard day, a brisk walk in the park and so on. After just a few experiences in meditation, tasting my very essence as peace, I realised very quickly how much I had been fooling myself in trying to extract peace from the world around me or even from some physical sensation in my own body.

I started to see physical relaxation as an escape from tension, and not a solution for it, and the beautiful scenes of nature now no longer as sources radiating peace. But in fact it was their mere absence of conflict, their harmony of colours, forms and sounds which had appealed to me, appealed because there was something in me which cried out also to be free from conflict. I discovered that 'small voice' or need was only my true nature demanding to be recognised. I saw that neither the body nor nature could give the peace that the soul was yearning for, that it had to be tapped from within. Having found it, it remains constant, whether in the city or countryside, in comfort or discomfort. In the midst of noise and confusion, peace is really my own.'

Meditation

Yoga in a general sense means a mental connection or union, achieved through remembrance. Wherever the mind is focused, that can be called yoga. Whenever someone or something is remembered, then the soul is having yoga with that person or thing. At any moment, we are remembering people, places and things of the past or present, or we are imagining future events. We are continually using this power within as we use the world outside, trying to find and maintain peace and happiness. We like to remember pleasant experiences and to entertain them as thoughts. We become 'lost' in thought, detached from our immediate surroundings and problems. It is a natural ability of the soul to withdraw into itself in the face of external difficulties.

The same ability is used in meditation. The intellect, as the receptacle of knowledge, is what understands and remembers too. Within the soul, the intellect wanders into the past *sanskaras*; then, what was initially a decision to remember someone or something, becomes thought. As long as the intellect remains fixed on the person or thing, the soul experiences its qualities. For example, when we remember a beautiful summer experience of relative peace and quiet, we re-experience the scenes, forget our problems and drift away. If we remember something painful or unpleasant, or someone's faults, the mind is disturbed. The mind experiences different states according to the types of thoughts that arise. The thoughts depend on where the intellect is focused. In short, as is the consciousness so is the experience.

Raja Yoga, the highest yoga, or remembrance, works entirely on the level of mind, intellect and *sanskaras,* rather than focusing on bodily forms, postures or rituals. The first stage in Raja Yoga is to stabilise the self in the pure experience of the inner tranquillity of the soul. At first, distracting thoughts may come to the mind. To be free from these, do not become involved in a struggle to contain or eradicate these wasteful thoughts, but merely step away from them.

Meditation experience

Whenever the situation or atmosphere becomes polluted with tension, sorrow or negativity of any description, withdraw immediately into the self and dive deep into the ocean of positive *sanskaras,* picking up the pearls of peace and contentment. Come back to that situation feeling refreshed, calm and clear, with the strength to deal with any circumstances. The process of self-introspection need only take a few moments.

Experiencing the Self

Let the intellect focus on the following thoughts and reading over them slowly, go deeply into the experience of each state being described: *The soul is weightless and light... Let the intellect see deeply into the self and remember the stillness of the original state... Let the outside world continue on its way, and for a few moments be detached from it... Turn within, and enjoy the inner treasures... of calmness, of peace, a very pure experience... The peaceful soul can more easily gather together its store of inner powers... Peace itself is a rare power... Just sitting and feeling still, experience the refreshment and restoration of strength to the intellect... the cleansing of the mind.*

Atmosphere

Atmosphere could be written as *atma-sphere,* the sphere or environment around the soul. Just as the physical atmosphere is the result of climatic conditions and air quality, there is a subtle atmosphere which is not only sensed by but also influenced by the mind and analysed by the intellect. It is variously described as the 'prevailing mood', the 'vibration' and so on.

Expressions such as 'you could have cut the air with a knife' (describing the atmosphere in a room immediately after a heated conflict) refer to this subtle atmosphere which is not seen, heard or measured, but 'sensed' by the mind. The mood of excitement at political rallies and sporting functions, the horrible vibrations of hysterical passion and panic when a mob riots, the feeling of grief when a popular figure dies – on such occasions, only a strong soul can resist being affected by the atmosphere. What is the cause of this non-physical atmosphere, these 'vibrations'?

Thoughts as energy

Thought has been proven to be a powerful yet non-physical 'energy', which can influence other souls and also matter. On a limited scale, there are experiments with ESP and mental telepathy. On a more sensational level, some use the power of thought to such an extent that steel objects can be bent and heavy objects moved without any physical aid. In the case of telepathy, communication over thousands of miles is possible in an instant when two souls are 'tuned' to each other's mental 'wavelength', as if the broadcasting and receiving of thoughts form some sort of subtle radio system. Occult powers also invoke the power of thought, although often for impure or egoistic motives and gains. The Emperor Napoleon made sure the battle was won in his mind before he entered the battlefield. Thought can be regarded as the energy or subtle force which links the soul to physical matter through the soul's connection with the body.

Thoughts, emotions, desires and moods generate a 'field' around the soul which, just like an electric field, can be called positive, negative or neutral, depending on the quality of its effect on other souls and on matter. When a large number of souls are all experiencing the same emotion, then the atmosphere becomes 'charged' with it. The large frenzied mob, gripped in panic, generates a powerful sinister atmosphere, more so than a person experiencing the same emotion on his own. Similarly, a soul with great mental power or talents generates 'charisma', which is really just a more powerful vibration than a weaker soul.

Creating a powerful atmosphere

Without the benefit of a powerful intellect, a weak soul is at the mercy of the atmosphere. Whatever the atmosphere, so will be the emotions and thoughts evoked from the *sanskaras,* whether the person enjoys that emotion or not. At such times it is impossible to escape from the effect of the atmosphere. When a soul is so dependent, it is unable to choose its thoughts or draw from its *sanskaras* any desired experience.

To be detached from a negative atmosphere and to be instrumental in creating a powerful, positive atmosphere, the soul must:
• pay powerful attention to its own true nature
• use the intellect to clear the mind and become introspective
• look deep into the self and choose the purer, more elevated human emotions of peace, power, contentment or whatever quality is needed and retain that in the mind.

Instead of expecting situations always to be giving some personal benefit, the soul should see how it could give benefit in any situation, thus creating a powerful atmosphere of benefit. Where there is expectation, there is always the possibility of disappointment; but where there is an attitude of giving benefit, there can never be disappointment.

When the soul has the power to maintain its chosen positive experience in the mind, it generates a powerful, pure atmosphere. The more powerful the soul, and the greater the number of other souls experiencing the same thoughts, the more powerful the corresponding atmosphere.

The original nature of the soul is to be peaceful. Through Raja Yoga, we develop the power to maintain an experience of peace for long periods, even when speaking or performing action, and this very naturally has an effect on the immediate atmosphere, wherever we may be: in a room, a lift, a bus, on the street. Ultimately I can affect the entire world in a positive way.

Chapter 2 Soul-Consciousness – the Gateway to God

'I am a peaceful soul'

Some think that everything in this world is unreal or an illusion (*Maya*) but this is not so. The drama, the stage, the actors and the roles are real enough, but it is our vision of things, and our deductions, that can be illusory. The basic illusion, 'I am a body', is like a thread running through the existence of the majority, on which all other thoughts, decisions and actions are strung.

The eternal soul, believing itself to be finite with a beginning and end, gives birth to myriad illusory desires and to such psychological insecurity that it tries to protect or support itself with scaffolding comprising the five main negative forces: anger, greed, ego, lust and attachment. The soul confuses itself by basing its total self-identification on the physical body: 'I am so-and-so, the son of so-and so, the resident of such-and-such a place, of this or that religion or race; I am in such a profession, of this age' and so on. Through these thoughts, which are the natural offspring of the thought, 'I am a body', the eternal soul becomes trapped in a world of temporary illusions, likes and dislikes.

The actor (the soul) doesn't only believe that it is the costume (the body), but also the role that it is playing. Thus, this ego-sense or body-consciousness doesn't only restrict the soul to its form but to its name as well. While the soul remains a prisoner of its own role and form, it can't see the wider aspects of the drama of life in which it is involved. It remains restricted to the conditions of each place, moment and circumstance, bound by past habits and attitudes. If the situation is in harmony with the soul, it feels good; if not, it feels dejected and finds ways to escape from the imaginary or real threats of that situation. In this way, the soul passes from one scene to another, like a piece of cork on the high seas at the mercy of its own destiny. The soul in body-consciousness cannot control its own movements, but they are imposed by the external conditions, which the soul itself is continually determining, according to the law of cause and effect *(see Chapter 4)*. Lost in the waves of attractions and repulsions, restricted thus by the name and form of its body, the soul feeds and is fed by many illusions: 'I'll stay with you; you'll give me everything I want from life', 'I want to eat, see, hear, taste and feel this and that, because these things will give me what I want.' Such desires are endless.

The door that opens to the world of spiritual knowledge and inculcation of positive qualities is the thought: 'I am a peaceful soul.' This thought, created with the understanding of its implications, is the most powerful and pure thought possible. It is this thought that immediately stills the restless mind and creates the stability necessary to absorb spiritual knowledge and power. It is this thought, too, that channels the soul's potential for good. Just as a river, when properly harnessed, provides life for many, so, too, the properly harnessed mind provides a reservoir that can serve to uplift others. Just as an uncontrolled river causes floods, the ungoverned mind causes damage to the self and to others.

The consideration and concentration on worldly things, though obviously necessary, does not fill the soul with the bliss it seeks. By concentrating on understanding the atom, scientists have unleashed the power within it. Similarly, by concentrating with love on the soul and its eternal bond with the Supreme Soul, we can unleash our own potential and pure power.

What is consciousness?

The soul is conscient energy, aware of its own existence. Consciousness can be described as the feeling 'I am' or 'I exist'. If you examine any thought-decision-action process, you will find that behind it, there is always the feeling: 'I am something or the other.' Consciousness is thus the springboard for thoughts, decisions and actions. In other words, the soul reacts to external circumstances according to how it regards itself at that particular moment.

For example, a surgeon is able to perform surgery when there is the consciousness of being a surgeon. That very consciousness unlocks or gives the soul access to all the information and experience related to being a surgeon. The soul, when it has the consciousness of being a soul, is able to have instant access to its own original qualities. As we have discussed, there are two different basic levels of consciousness: 'I am a body' or 'I am a soul', the former, illusory, and the latter, real. When the feeling is 'I am a body', the thought process is trapped in the limitations, problems and vision of the physical identity. Its reaction to others is on the same level.

The following table shows the difference in the case of a typical parent–child relationship.

BODY-CONSCIOUSNESS	SOUL-CONSCIOUSNESS
AWARENESS I am the parent; I know more than my child. After all, I'm older and wiser.	I am a spiritual being. I have to play out a role of responsibility. Each of my children has his/her own specific role.
THOUGHT They should listen to me. After all, I am the one who bears the burden.	Let me listen to their suggestions. Perhaps we can improve our communication.
DECISION I will show them who is in charge here.	Let me understand each child's specialities.
ACTION The parent shouts and argues with the child.	A two-way dialogue ensues.
RESULT Ill-feeling between parent and child.	Respect and a climate of love and trust is fostered.

This example clearly demonstrates the benefits of having a soul-conscious relationship or, in other words, seeing the other as a soul and not as a body.

Body-consciousness – the cause of mental tension

Since there is such disparity between the body and the soul, it is essential to realise this if one strives for peace of mind. It is not the body that desires peace; it is the soul. It is not the body that has a relationship with God; it is the soul.

When a soul leaves its body there is a distinct separation between matter and spirit. In understanding death we can better understand life.

Moreover, would it not be better to experience the benefits of such self-realisation in one's practical life now? Can you imagine a driver thinking that she is the car, or a guest thinking he is the hotel? This is exactly what has happened. The soul has become totally identified with its housing. People think: 'I AM a body and I HAVE a soul.' In reality, the contrary is true: 'I AM a soul and I HAVE a body.'

In the following thoughts we can easily see the seeds of all types of prejudice, whether sexual, national, racial, religious, social, age:

I am female	You are male
I am Russian	You are American
I am white	You are black
I am Christian	You are Muslim
I am rich	You are poor
I am old	You are young

The body-conscious soul thus classifies the world, has desires, adopts a perspective and responds, according to its limited vision. The insecurity that this brings then manifests as anger, greed, ego, lust or attachment of some type or another. If you examine deeply what causes sorrow, you will see it is due to the mis-identification of the true self with one's physical identity and roles. In this state, the mental process is a slave of the body and the external situation. The car becomes the controller of the driver.

The soul, because it is a soul and not a body, becomes insecure and tries to compensate with material things, status, profession, relationships, and so on, which, while appearing to give comfort and safety, in fact become further sources of worry and depression. Lust is the search for security through possessions or selfish relationships. Greed is the search for security through the accumulation of things, money, status and keeping one's stomach always full. Ego is the search for security through the wearing of many masks related to the roles that one has to play. Anger is the guard which tries to protect the false sense of security when any of the other four are threatened. Armed with a bevy of harsh words and actions, anger patrols the walls of the castle of illusions built in body-consciousness.

Just as the cobra has a diamond shape in the centre of the forehead, we should transform the habit of seeing the 'skin' or body classification of others into seeing the diamond, the soul, in the centre of the forehead.

Each person is our family member. We are all visitors to this earth. We are all actors in this world drama. Each 'I' is a soul. The soul has no sex,

IN BODY-CONSCIOUSNESS	IN SOUL-CONSCIOUSNESS
I am in bondage.	There are no bondages; I am free.
I have many questions and few answers.	I understand everything that I do.
I am afraid of dying (losing the body).	I know I am eternal and there is no fear of death.
I have no control over the sense organs.	I am able to practise self-control.
I become bored and depressed easily.	I understand situations and overcome them easily. I'm able to maintain enthusiasm.
The wings of the soul are clipped.	I have wings of thought to fly beyond the body.
The intellect is dull.	The intellect is sharp.
I am limited to the perception of this world.	I can travel to other regions beyond this world.
I see a distorted past and have no clear aim for the future.	The past, present and future of my part in Drama are seen clearly.
I am disturbed by feelings of attraction and lust for bodies.	I am attracted by the qualities of the Supreme Soul only.
I give sorrow, like a thorn hurting everyone.	I spread the fragrance of virtues like a flower.
I see everyone relative to my identity, my life revolving around 'me'...This is arrogance.	I respect all individuals and relate to them with humility.
I am tense and tired.	I am alert and relaxed.

nationality or race. In this way we will see not only our own true value, but the true value of others and the true value of this world around us.

In soul-consciousness, the soul is in its rightful place as ruler of the body, sitting on its throne between the eyebrows. Soul-consciousness also refers to being aware of one's own original state. In body-consciousness, the soul sees a problem as a huge mountain; in soul-consciousness, the soul sees the same problem as a tiny mound. The problem is the same, but the new perspective has reduced the worry or fear involved to nothing.

The original home

Birth-Life-Death-Rebirth

The realisation of the self as a soul, an eternal entity, naturally leads to the questions:
- Where is the soul before it comes into a physical body?
- Where does the soul go after it leaves it?
- What is the purpose of eternity?

These are questions that deeply concern human beings. Yet, until now, proof of life before birth or after death has been inconclusive. The images conjuring up the 'fires of hell' and a heavenly world beyond the clouds have figured greatly in the world's religions. Yet, to the rationally-minded, the states of living forever, tormented in sulphurous pits, or conversely, lounging in perpetual bliss in a fairy-tale kingdom, seem far removed from the reality of the present.

Most accept that there is some order to the creation but, viewing our drama through spectacles of body-consciousness, it is impossible to see it, as the soul is imprisoned by bodily needs and sensual desires. In body-consciousness the soul is unable to see anything objectively. Only when confronted by death does one instinctively consider 'life after death'. At funerals, everyone faces the new absence of a loved person, the departure of the personality and the impermanence of the body.

Everyone wishes that the departed one will go to 'heaven' and not to 'hell'. We subconsciously know that we are souls. Birth, life and death are just stages in existence. In fact, all natural processes can be found to have a beginning, a middle, an end and a new beginning to continue the cycle. The soul takes a bodily form, gives life to it and after a period of time, long or short, leaves it and takes another suited to the continuation of its role. As long as the soul is in the body, the body grows like a plant from baby to child, youth to maturity. It then begins to decay and finally becomes unserviceable. The moment the soul leaves the body, it becomes like a dead log. It immediately starts to decompose and eventually goes back 'to dust'.

Again, the soul moves into a foetus. After some time it emerges as a newborn baby and immediately begins to show the tendencies and characteristics it had developed in its previous life. It is the same soul but in a new physical situation. Thus death is merely the means by which a complete change of circumstances and environment for the soul takes place. Time never kills the soul, but the body, being a part of nature or matter, obeys the law of decay that everything new becomes old and eventually ceases to hold its form. The molecular components of this body disintegrate only to re-integrate as another form some time later.

The process of birth-life-death-rebirth is also eternal. It has always been going on and will continue. The soul comes into the body, expresses a role and experiences the results of that for a certain time, then leaves it and the process starts again. Similarly, souls come into this world, remain here as actors for a number of lifetimes and then return to the region from which they come, for rest. This process also starts again. The pattern is a cyclic one.

Why does the soul search for peace, love and happiness?

The search for true values is a constant preoccupation. In body-consciousness we mistakenly think that the physical world and physical relations can provide peace, love and happiness. However these are not the properties of matter, nor of the physical identity, but the true characteristics of the soul. This has to be realised.

Imagine that you are surrounded by all your favourite things: food, music, fragrance, scenery and companions. As you are about to enjoy your meal, the telephone rings and you are told that a person close to you has just died. Instantly, that scene of 'favourites' melts into an insipid and superficial experience. Something has happened that shakes the soul and it can no longer enjoy those things. At the same time it finds itself inadequate in the face of the bad news, as understanding and power are missing. Life is full of experiences such as this and it becomes clear that physical things are not the sources of peace, love and happiness, but that understanding and inner strength are.

One of the basic facts of human psychology is that we do not seek or desire something that has not been experienced previously. For example, if one has never tasted a mango, there cannot be a burning desire to have a mango. This suggests that desires might arise from previous life experiences. In fact, it is impossible for a human being to act or desire

29

outside the field of his or her own experience. The search for peace, love and happiness is so fundamental to the human spirit because these are the original and true qualities of the soul itself.

This world and the regions beyond

The physical world

This world is a vast amphitheatre of action in which embodied souls play their respective and various parts. Planet Earth exists in an extremely tiny portion of the physical universe and is governed by well-defined physical, chemical and biological laws.

In India, the world which we inhabit is called *karma kshetra* (the field of action), because it is here that we sow the seeds of actions and reap their fruits. It is here that the soul takes on flesh and bones and expresses the role that it has latent within itself, causing variations in the material environment. The state of the material world at any given moment is a direct reflection of the state of consciousness of the human beings which inhabit it. If there is peace and harmony within the soul, this is reflected in nature. If there is conflict and confusion, nature responds accordingly.

It is a world of three dimensions of space and one of time. Its principal characteristics are sound, movement, colour and form. On this immense stage of deserts, forests, mountains and seas, illuminated by the sun, moon and stars, the drama of existence is enacted. In the drama, the actor-souls are subject to dualities: from pleasure to pain, birth to death, purity to impurity, happiness to sorrow, new to old, positive to negative. The vast pageant of history crawls along as indefatigable time devours all. A point is finally reached when the process is renewed and all souls and the elements of matter themselves move back to their points of origin, only to start again.

The regions beyond

Beyond the limits of this vast expanse of the solar system and galaxies there are regions of non-material light. They are not reached by any physical means because it is simply not a question of light years or kilometres. They are regions which 'transcend' the physical plane and therefore can only be experienced through divine vision, perceivable to the *third eye*. Through deep meditation the soul can 'travel' to these regions and experience the bliss of being free from the limits of anything earthly.

The subtle regions

These regions are like three subtle 'layers' around the physical plane which are absolutely necessary for the roles of creation, its sustenance and the destruction of the old and impure. Thus they have an important part in world transformation. (This part will be explained in Chapter 6.) Those who have the gift of divine trance are able to have a vision of these regions. Such souls see the scenes much in the same manner as one experiences a dream but much more vividly. Since the bodies there are of light and not matter, there is movement but no sound. The scenes perceived in trance are like silent movies in which communication is by gesture and thought.

The soul world – the home

Further beyond the subtle regions is another region. It is pervaded by golden-red, divine light, which is the sixth element called *brahm*. It is the region from which all souls have descended onto this earth. The conscient entities, the souls, have neither bodies of matter nor bodies of light. There exists neither thought, word nor action; there is just complete stillness, silence and peace. Just as this world occupies a tiny part of this physical universe, so too the souls occupy just a tiny portion of this infinite golden-red light.

This is the highest region, the original home of souls and the Supreme Soul, God. This is the region which human beings, irrespective of culture or religion, have tried to reach in thoughts, prayers and so on. It is called *heaven* by Christians, *Nirvana* by Buddhists, *Shantidham, Paramdham* or *Brahmand* by Hindus. Before I came to this earth, I was there with all other souls, my brothers. The experience of complete and utter peace, purity and silence is there in my sweet home. There the soul is untainted by matter. Souls abide there as star-like points of light. They remain dormant, with their roles in the physical world merged or latent within them.

The souls stay in the soul world in well-defined groups. They descend onto this earth in a certain chronological order, according to the quality of *sanskaras*. At the apex of this configuration of souls is the Supreme Soul, whom the other souls call variously: God, Allah, Jehovah, Shiva and so on. Beneath Him the souls are positioned numberwise according to their degree of similarity to God. Depending on the quality and the part the soul has to play, it emerges in the human world, taking the body of a developing baby in a mother's womb. It then continues through the cycle of birth and rebirth, according to the role that it has. When the parts are over, souls again return to this world of light, peace, liberation and complete purity.

The deep rest the soul has had in the 'home' has such an effect on it that, even though it forgets the details about that world, there is always the impetus to search for that peace and silence when it becomes lost and confused in the world of matter. In that supreme region only, souls remain in their completely original, natural state, which can be experienced through Raja Yoga meditation.

What has happened to the original nature of the soul?

I, the soul, am originally a starlike point of perfect peace and purity, twinkling in the golden-red expanse of the soul world. I am fully charged with spiritual energy which naturally manifests as love, joy, peace and purity when I first come into this physical world. Gradually, by taking many births, I become attached to the senses and the various sense objects and I forget my original attributes. Then I become a slave to five basic negative forces: anger, greed, ego, lust and attachment. These forces have their roots in body-consciousness, or the illusion that existence is entirely physical. My ability to control matter is supplanted by matter is controlling me. Any time I suffer disappointment, worry or anxiety, it is due to the effect of any one of these negative influences.

I forget the heights of spiritual attainment and the delights of super-sensuous joy, thinking myself to be a body, and I search for peace and happiness through the sense organs. I mistakenly pursue worldly pleasures in an effort to regain my former state. I forget my true identity, nature, home and my Supreme Father. I know that, while controlled by these negative forces, I cannot come back to my normal state of peace, happiness and bliss. These vices are unwelcome intruders into my original texture of purity. They are not welcome in my internal 'house'. Until the vices have no control over the soul, I will never restore my original qualities of peace, bliss, love, purity and knowledge.

People afflicted by anger lose their temper and become excited at the slightest provocation. Yet, when the event is over, they find 'peace' in reverting to their normal temperament. The same applies to all the other vices which are at the root of all emotional disturbances, strains, tensions and imbalances.

If I contemplate my original nature and do everything with the realisation 'I am a soul and not a body', my original qualities reappear naturally. They are my basic attributes. It is worthless seeking them externally. It is like the musk deer running after the sweet smell of musk, unaware that it is coming from its own navel. Peace of mind is my property. It automatically flows from within me once I am soul-conscious.

I only have to let my original *sanskaras* become thoughts and keep them flowing. Whatever thoughts are in my mind, that is the state I experience. Soul-conscious thoughts bring peace of mind. Body-conscious thoughts disturb me. It is I who decide what state of mind to experience. I can either be the essence of peace, or in a turmoil. It is I, the soul, who has the power of decision. The situation should not dictate to me. Soul-consciousness is the mind's food that strengthens the intellect and keeps me beyond the influence of negativity.

Raja Yoga meditation – regaining the awareness

As was explained in the last chapter, meditation is not a process of emptying the mind of thought. It uses the natural endowment of the soul – thought – as a take-off point into the consciousness of the true self. I climb a well-prepared ladder of thoughts and eventually climb beyond it into the pure experience of what I really am.

Churning over these pure and real thoughts can occupy the soul for long periods of time. The deeper significances of Raja Yoga will be unfolded but, on the basis of what has been discussed so far, you will be able to experience the self as a soul and discover some of your unique potential powers. First comes the realisation: I am a soul; I am mind, intellect and *sanskaras*. My ears, eyes, nose, mouth are just the organs through which I can enjoy life. It is due to body-consciousness and the build up of past negative *sanskaras* that I have been trapped by these five vices: anger, greed, ego, lust and attachment. I now possess the knowledge that will free me from my cage. I have the key. I am a soul, 'a bird'. Knowing this, I am not bound by physical laws. I can detach and fly at the speed of a thought, to the soul world, where I can easily experience my original state. I must realise that it is impossible to have 'peace of mind' if I cannot have detachment from the body.

During the initial stages of meditation many wasteful thoughts do come. This is due to the soul's long standing habit of thinking aimlessly. The mind has been attracted or repelled by everything and everyone. The soul has been buffeted around from one experience to another, one scene to another. I must break the negative cycles of worry, doubt and confusion within, by recharging the soul with my own original attributes of peace, purity, love and joy. I must make sure the engines of my senses are not burning up the vital fuel of inner peace.

The soul does not grow or diminish but only experiences change in its happiness or unhappiness, peace or peacelessness. The use of the word 'peaceless', suggests that I was at some stage peaceful. I now know that I had peace in the soul world. I can see how peace is the real 'oxygen' for the soul. When I do not have it, I choke and gasp and look for it everywhere. I must look upon all my relatives, friends, associates as souls also coming from the soul world. We are all fellow souls.

Raja Yoga meditation is a means to channel good thought energy into one's moods. It means to turn the thoughts away from those of anger, greed and frustration to a far higher level of peace and contentment.

Is it possible to control the flow of thoughts?

Before doing any action we first have to think. Yet how much time do we spend, developing the thinking faculty, the mind? With a little knowledge of the power of thought and soul-consciousness, I can remove all inner storms and enjoy a tranquil existence. With knowledge I can control any mood, which brings enormous benefit both to myself and to all others with whom I have contact.

As was stated, we spend most of our time searching externally for fulfilment. This means that the soul is totally at the mercy of what is going on externally. If the scene is unpleasant, or even if something very minor goes wrong, I become worried and upset. Through the practice of soul-consciousness and meditation, I can remain strong and content, come what may. I am a soul and I have my own store of peace from which I can draw at any time. I do not need to practise complicated breathing exercises or strenuous physical posturing. I can draw on my own experience of just being a soul wherever I am, in the countryside or in the city, at home or at work. So, meditation can be a continuing experience rather than a static one.

The understanding of the self as a soul is the foundation of all spiritual experience. If you have practised some form of meditation before, it is likely that you were asked to concentrate on a flower, a dot on the wall, the picture of some great saint, a candle-flame or maybe even to repeat endlessly some words which are little understood. To concentrate, I must have a focus that is certain and easy to visualise. Very simply and naturally, I, the soul, on the wings of my thoughts can fly to my eternal and highest home and experience my original attributes.

As I begin to practise soul-consciousness, I learn to detach myself from the diverse and difficult situations around me and turn naturally to my home and the Father of all souls who dwells there. The mind becomes automatically controlled by this flow of peace. With the fundamental understanding of the distinctions between soul and body, the spiritual and the physical, I begin to meditate.

Meditation exercises

Read the following words slowly and go into the experience of each suggested thought.

Remembering the self as a soul and not a body
What is the 'I'?
I am a soul... I am the life force... I am the driver... I, the soul,... a tiny star, have no size... I am really just a pinpoint of light... I can easily detach from the world around me... From my throne between my brows, I am the ruler of all my sense organs... I feel far away from the problems of the day... I am just a peaceful soul,... loveful soul,... All others are souls like me... all tiny shining stars... All are my fellow souls... I feel far away from the physical world... I am just a soul,... mind, intellect and a set of personality traits... I am peaceful...

Remembering the home of the soul
I am a soul... My attention is now focused totally on this... No longer does the physical world pull on my thoughts... On the screen of my mind, I picture my destination,... a world of light beyond the sun and the stars,... a region of soft and subtle, golden-red light... On the wings of thought I fly there,.... leaving the physical world behind... My destination is clear... I see myself,... a pure sparkling star,... shining... I experience my natural original qualities of peace, love, power, joy... I recognise this world,... my sweet home,...total stillness,...total silence... I am just a pure, peaceful star,...radiating love in my sweet home...I remember this home so well... I feel completely natural... The physical world is far away... I am just a tiny spark, radiating peace in my sweet home of golden-red light... Since leaving here so many births ago, I have been trying to find my way back here... Now I am here,... full of peace,... full of love,... full of contentment.

Remembering the original state of the soul

I am so far away from the world of bodies, burdens, problems,... from the limitations of matter,... just a sparkling star, floating freely in my sweet home,... enjoying the original experience of purity,... peace,... joy,... complete freedom,... absolutely nothing weighing on the soul... Here I was and am again... after so long,... full of peace,... still,... silent... I go into the experience of my original qualities.

Chapter 3 God

Meditation

The first stage of meditation is to stabilise the mind in the remembrance of the soul: 'I am a soul acting through the body.' Then the intellect goes deep into the *sanskaras* and brings out the powerful *sanskaras* of peace and purity. To enable this practice to become a constant experience, the intellect must become stronger. Knowledge alone is not sufficient. The second stage of meditation is concentration. This concentration refines and sharpens the powers of the intellect. Concentration has been described as holding the mind to one thought so that it becomes the shape of that thought.

Raja Yoga means to collect together the scattered forces of one's thoughts, establish them in the real self and then connect with the Supreme Soul. Initially, when an aspirant begins to practise Raja Yoga, it can be difficult to concentrate the mind on the self and God for more than a few seconds because thoughts are easily distracted. This naturally happens. During the initial attempts, the moments of concentration are bound to be few, short and erratic, but even a single moment of concentration is invaluable because it gives a taste of that inner bliss which sustains further concentration. This should be treated as a period of test and trial.

Past *sanskaras* will come to the surface. Thoughts of one's physical identity and burdens will create hurdles. Any attempt to drive them out will merely encourage them more intensely. The aspirant should take it cheerfully and sublimate the intruding thoughts by contemplation on points of knowledge. When the mind experiences a flow of powerful, pure thoughts, then the pure experience of the soul's qualities is possible.

Some yoga practitioners try forcibly to create a mental void, by driving out all thoughts in an attempt to control the negative and superfluous ones. Such a mental vacuum is only temporary and expels the good thoughts along with the bad ones. Pure thoughts are nourishment for the soul which leads to the practical realisation of knowledge.

Concentration on God

Concentration on the form and attributes of God fulfils all the requirements of meditation. It becomes natural and easy when there is a relationship with Him. This chapter discusses the name, form, abode, attributes and acts of God, the understanding of which enables the maintenance of a natural link during meditation practice.

Who is God and what is my relationship with Him?

This is a question that, for the vast majority, remains unanswered and therefore the experience of God remains unfulfilled. Yet the concepts about God are as varied as are the *sanskaras* of human beings. Some say God is everywhere; some say He is nowhere. Some say He created everything out of nothing, or expanded everything out of Himself; others see that as an illogical impossibility. Many say God is beyond the comprehension of limited human intellects; others believe that they have understood Him and are revered as 'self-realised' beings. Still others believe themselves to be God and allow themselves to be worshipped.

Some say that God creates only what is good, and others say that God also creates evil, and that everything is just 'God's play'. God is seen by some to be the mere expression of human beings' needs and that they will soon evolve beyond needing such a figure-head. Some say He makes the grass grow and the wind blow; others say He is merely the 'voice of the conscience' – the 'inner voice'. Others define God as the higher self who remains constantly at peace; this conceptualisation is called 'cosmic-consciousness', since the one with this attribute is said to be 'at one with the whole universe'.

There is an endless stream of human theories and concepts which appear to create confusion and ill-feeling when they are opposed to each other, but ultimately I must ask myself how far 'I', the individual, have the experience of His powers and qualities.

The basis of forming a relationship with anyone is knowledge of who they are, what they look like, where they are from and what they do. Similarly, if I am to have the awareness of myself as a soul, and, stemming from that, a close relationship with God, the Supreme Soul, then I must know:

Who He is
What His form is
Where He is
What His attributes are
What His acts are
Where I stand in relationship to Him

God is living and real and not a matter of theological speculation. It is necessary for me to re-establish a living contact with Him, on the basis of knowledge of Him. My connection should not be based on the fears and superstitions of the past.

Universal concepts of God

There are some universally accepted attributes of God.
God is the creator and preserver.
God is the highest.
God is the Supreme Father.
God is non-physical.
God is omnipotent.
God is a conscient being.
God is all-loving, all-knowing.
God is immutable.
God is one and God is light.
God is morally perfect.
God is absolutely just.
God is the Supreme Benefactor.
God is the saviour of souls.
God is the purifier.
God is mysterious in His ways.

Even in polytheistic religions, there is one God who stands above the others. Monotheistic faiths believe God to be one single Supreme Being. Traditions, sacred texts, monuments, sayings and rituals all over the world point to the existence of and belief in one knowledgeable, all-powerful and merciful being. That being is universally prayed to and recognised as the remover of sorrow, the giver of happiness and the redeemer of the 'sinful'.

Form of God

We have recognised that God is infinite and unlimited. Infinity is usually connected with vastness. However, it has another aspect, which is beyond geometrical dimension or infinitesimal, ie no size. As has been stated, God is a soul. As a soul, He has the same form as human souls. The only difference is in the qualities and not in the size. We have rightly thought that God is great, but His greatness doesn't mean that He is expanded throughout the entire universe. The power of a soul has no connection with its physical dimensions at all.

On the one hand, people say God is formless and on the other, they say He is omnipresent, ie all forms, which means practically the same. Anything that exists must have a form. Qualities indeed are formless, but the source of those qualities cannot be without form. For example, fragrance has no form but the flower does. The sun has form but the light and warmth it radiates do not. God has form but the qualities radiating from Him do not. In other words, God is not love but the source of love; God is not truth but the source of truth, and so on. If He is formless, then communication with Him is impossible. The very word *yoga* implies a meeting between two entities.

God is a microstar, just as I am. Knowing God's form, I can bring that image onto the screen of my mind and begin immediately to experience His powers and qualities by associating them with that beautiful form. There is much more value in meditating on God's form and attributes than in focusing for example on one's breath, candle-flames and so on.

Evidence from the world's religions

From this spark of light emanates an oval aura, just as a candle-flame emerges from a point source and assumes an oval form. Mystics and saints throughout the ages have had visions of God as this point of self-luminous light with an oval aura.

Most religions have images, idols or memorials, bearing one name or the other, to represent God as light or as an oval shape. Throughout India there are statues of an oval-shaped image. They are called *Shivalingas* and are thought to represent the seed of fertility, but actually they represent the Creator Himself. The names of the temples of Shiva attest to this: Somnath, the Lord of Nectar; Vishwanath, the Lord of the Universe; Mukteshwara, the Lord of Liberation.

God

In the *Old Testament* Moses had a vision of light as a 'burning' bush in the desert. Jacob, after having a dream-vision of a ladder to heaven, with angels ascending and descending, took the stone he was using for a pillow, set it upright and poured oil onto it in adoration. It was oval-shaped. St Paul had a vision of light while on the road to Damascus. Jesus referred to God as light, while Guru Nanak, the founder of Sikhism called Him *Ek Omkar*, the one Incorporeal Being. In some Christian ceremonies, during the proceedings, an ostensorio is held up. It is a golden ball with many rays emanating from it. Perhaps this is a symbolic representation of God.

According to Islamic legend, when Adam left paradise he came to a low hill upon which he saw a shining white oval stone. Around this stone he circled seven times praising God. He then built the Kaaba. By the time of Abraham it needed to be rebuilt as a temple to honour the one God.

The town of Mecca grew around this spot. This oval stone, later called Sang-e-aswad and now 'blackened' by the kisses of millions of sinners, so they say, is the only object of worship in the whole of Islam.

The Zoroastrians worship God as fire. The ancient Egyptians worshipped the sun as God. A Buddhist sect in Japan focuses the mind on a small oval shape. They call it *Karni,* the Peace-giver. The Jews have the *Menorah* which, when lit, is a memory of this form.

It seems therefore that human beings, without realising, have all been worshipping and trying to discover the same God. There is only one God and His form is light. If union between the soul and the Supreme Soul is to take place, it can only be possible if there is knowledge of that form.

Name of God

What has a form also has a name. So too, God has a name. There are more names for God than there are languages, and each name highlights one of His specialities. The sanskrit word *'Shiva'* describes His eternal attributes and functions. It means benefactor father, the seed of creation and point source, and implies that there can be no other creator above Him.

The word *Shiva* is an introduction to God, but, in meditation, Indians adjoin another word: *'Baba'* or 'Father' ('Daddy' or 'Dad') which conveys the closeness and sweetness of the relationship. So the words *'Shiva Baba'* convey His role and my relationship with Him. *Shiva* is not to be confused with the figure of Hindu mythology who is also called *Shankar.*

Abode of God

Where does God live? Is there somewhere I can go to see Him, to be with Him? Since God is a tiny starlike soul, it is obvious that He does not pervade the physical universe. In fact, He is beyond it. He is in one location, and, when I discover that location, I can send my mind to Him wherever I am and whatever I am doing.

The 'home' of the soul and the Supreme Soul is the region of subtle, golden-red light, which can be visualised during meditation. It doesn't mean that He is millions of light years away. I can reach Him in one thought, just as a correctly dialled telephone number connects me. He is only one thought distant from me. In this region of absolute stillness, silence and purity, God, the Supreme Soul, is able to remain perfectly stable, constant and unchanging, while the rest of the universe and the souls are changing around Him. The Father's home is also that of the children. Some people think that God dwells in the heart of human beings. In a figurative way He does, through love. What we think to be God within us is really the eternal and unforgettable impression of Him. His real home is the soul world.

Attributes of God

On the basis of our similarities of form and abode, I learn from God of my own original attributes of peace, purity, love, knowledge, power and bliss. As I tune my thoughts to Him, His influence brings out these original qualities in me. He is the perfect and infinite fountain, indeed, the ocean of these qualities. His superiority lies in the depth, clarity and continuity of His attributes. While human souls fluctuate between peace and peacelessness; love and conflict; knowledge and ignorance; agony and ecstasy, God is ever-constant. He remains beyond the fields of change and relativity and is beyond certain concepts held by human beings.

Omniscience

It is held that God knows the details of every atom and every thought in the universe.

It is because of God's ultimate, pervasive knowledge that He can be described as an ocean, whereas it is through ignorance and lack of understanding that human souls enter into sorrow. Understanding this world does not necessarily mean to be aware of every detail of the movement of every single leaf or every single molecule. All that is required is to understand the conditions through which things pass. One of the basic beliefs of Christians is that: 'In the beginning was the Word and the Word was with God and the Word was God...', which suggests that He is the embodiment of knowledge. It is believed that it was by the 'Word' that 'He created man in His own image'.

God creates with knowledge. Being the wisest of all, He has the power to change the intellects of human souls. By imparting to us the knowledge of Himself, the Creator, and the beginning, the middle and the end of creation, we are able to appreciate this vast world drama, and our true qualities of love, peace, bliss are touched. The laws of nature automatically take care of the details of nature, as the law of cause and effect *(karma)* takes care of the details of human life. In order for him to perform His work as Creator, it is not necessary for Him to listen to our every thought, our every secret. He is part of an eternal, predestined drama that He did not create but in which He finds Himself the principal actor.

Thus He is the only true altruist. Human actions, whether good or bad, are dictated by self-concern, whereas God has nothing to gain because He is complete in all respects. He is the perfect 'blueprint' of spirituality. He alone has the right to give knowledge regardless of human arguments. His knowledge is purely spiritual.

Omnipotence

All those who accept the reality of God believe that He is all-powerful. It is believed He can do anything and everything, that He is some sort of cosmic magician who, first, created this vast universe from nothing and continues to manipulate its workings whenever He chooses. It is thought that all that has been, is and will be is created and controlled by God. Some go so far as to say that the total cosmos is the mind of God. This has been a constant point of dispute.

Firstly, there are three distinct and eternal operative realities, each having its own powers and functions. There is God, there are souls and there is matter, or nature, together producing the scenes of creation.

Secondly, there are two fields of existence: the physical and the metaphysical. Both fields act, react and interact to produce this incredible, universal drama of which we are all a part, including God. Fundamentally, on the physical level there is the interaction between souls and matter which produces all phenomena. On the metaphysical level there is the interaction between souls and God, the remembering and forgetting of

Him, which gives the interesting plots and by-plots to the movement of events that we call world history.

Thirdly, 'eternal' implies that God neither created Himself, nor human souls, nor matter. As we more deeply understand the law of cause and effect (discussed in the next chapter), we can see the impossibility of God's being the literal physical Creator of this world and human beings. God, in fact, has no direct influence on nature. It is not He who throws lightning bolts at people, kills or grants babies, makes airplanes crash, causes earthquakes, floods and rainbows. This is the play between human souls and matter directly. The laws of nature are not the laws of God. The laws that human beings are following at this moment are not the laws of God. He teaches us His laws; we learn them, but forget them. God has been considered to be so great, so beyond comprehension, that some convenient automatic phrases have developed: 'It is the will of God... Everything is the will of God', or 'I'll be here next week, God willing.'

How can one say: 'God is beyond comprehension', and also say what His will is? The so-called sophisticates of the world laugh at the absurdity of a group of natives who believe that a volcanic explosion was the result of the wrath of an angry god within the mountain, while at the same time they try to explain such an explosion as an 'act of God'.

If God is an ocean of love, surely His will is the manifestation of that love. It is not His will to kill people, nor is it His power to bring them back to life. It is not He who makes the grass grow and the wind blow. It is not He who is the energy that binds the atoms together. It is not He who gives us our roles. It is because we have misunderstood His omnipotence that we seek His favour in the churches and temples: 'Grant us this...', 'God forgive me...' and so on. Though we flatter Him to give us this and that, when something goes wrong, or a relative dies, He is the one who is blamed. 'It is the will of God' is solemnly intoned by almost everyone.

There are certain immutable laws which govern the interplay of the soul, God and nature. God will not infringe those laws. He will not grant favours to some and not to others. Nor will He remove sin unless the devotee himself begins to make the efforts necessary. He is immune to both flattery and defamation.

God's greatness lies not in the ability to interfere with events when He chooses. It lies in the fact that He alone is the only one in the universe who upholds these laws perfectly and forever. His might is purely spiritual. The Supreme Father, Supreme Soul, uses His 'potency' for the benefit of the world. He uses His qualities to transform it when it reaches extreme degradation.

Human souls enter the world, and little by little, through birth and rebirth, lose some of their original powers through the contact with and influence of matter. Because of losing their qualities, matter starts to 'dominate' and defects and weaknesses appear in the soul, causing one to depend more and more on body-consciousness. Values change, virtues change into vices and the spiritual, and consequently physical, atmospheres become darker. In this obscurity, we rightly believe that God is the one who can help set things right.

God is not omnipresent

Is it really possible that the Supreme Soul pervades the entire universe?

The ancient sages of India used to say 'Neti neti' (it is not known), when asked about the identity of God, whereas their more recent counterparts have been claiming that God is everything and everywhere and even in human beings. The statement 'Nothing except God exists; He is everywhere' may reflect the heights of mystical poetry, but to interpret that as literal fact is another thing altogether. The feeling 'O Lord, wherever I am, Thou art with me…' certainly indicates a filial closeness between the soul and God but to twist the meaning of that into 'God is everywhere' is more than slightly unreasonable. The sun is in one place; yet its influence can be felt throughout the solar system to different degrees in different places, providing a source of heat and light, absolute essentials for our physical life. The closer one is to the sun, the greater the effect.

In the same way God, the one who is the ocean of perfect attributes, the source of all spiritual needs, does not have to be omnipresent in order to be with us wherever we are, because the feeling of closeness to God is something that is beyond physical dimensions.

If God were literally omnipresent and thus permeating every atom, where is this love, peace, joy and wisdom? Do they permeate every atom in this human world?

If I am pervaded by God, how could ignorance have come to me in the first place? Can ignorance come to God? If God is omnipresent, to where or to whom do I turn my thoughts?

Just as radio waves emanate throughout the world and a receiver, if tuned in, will pick them up, so too if the mind is tuned totally to the gross world and physical activities, then I am unable to experience God practically in my daily life. Even though He always radiates His qualities,

I can only pick up those transmissions if I am soul-conscious and if I turn my thoughts in His direction to His location. If God were omnipresent, there would be no meaning to the tradition throughout all cultures to have special places set aside (eg temples and churches) for worship. In those special places, is God more omnipresent than in other non-consecrated places? If God were omnipresent, are the ones who are so-called 'God-realised beings' more 'God' than the ones who have not realised?

If God were omnipresent, there would be no need for knowledge and no need to search for peace. The One who is the ocean of peace and the ocean of knowledge would be everywhere. Perhaps the strongest point against the idea of literal omnipresence is the point of relationship. In the heart of every soul the seal of truth is impressed: 'I am the child; God is my Father.'

God is also the supreme teacher, guide, liberator, friend and purifier of human souls. That is why all turn their thoughts to Him in their hours of despair. The idea that God is omnipresent is indeed the ultimate excuse and greatest escape from responsibility that human souls have made and continue to make. After all, if God were omnipresent, He would be responsible for good and evil.

An omnipresent God implies that we have nothing to complete in ourselves for we are already God. Am I really God? One could not seriously admit to such a claim.

Evidently it is the feeling that no matter where we are, God's presence can be felt, that is misunderstood. It is only through deep and concentrated meditation that one can enter the spiritual dimension where His presence is truly felt.

God, the creator, the law giver

Human souls created the present human systems, not God. When human beings infringe the natural laws to an extreme extent, it is the time for God to guide us back to the laws of harmony and righteousness. This is how He creates, not by some unexplained and inexplicable act of magic. On the basis of this knowledge, we recreate this world as it was.

God helps human souls by inspiring us to live within the parameters of natural law and empowers the soul to do it through Raja Yoga. His task as Creator is to purify souls when they have fallen into darkness and decay. It is His job because no one else has the knowledge, love or power to do it. He is the architect of the new world but it is we who are the builders.

It was a common belief among the ancient races that God was the source of all laws. The Aztecs' Supreme God, Taxcatlipocal, was said to have appeared on top of a mountain to reveal knowledge. The Cretans believed their law-giver ascended Mt Dicta and there received knowledge from the Supreme Lord, Zeus. The Egyptians venerated the laws which they deemed had been handed down by God via the secretary of mankind, Thoth. The ancient Hebrews and today's Jews and Christians believe that Yahweh, Jehovah, or God, handed down the Ten Commandments to Moses on Mt Sinai. The Zoroastrians believed that the Supreme God appeared to Zoroaster on a high mountain and delivered to him the *Zendavesta,* the *Book of the Law.*

There are many examples of similar patterns of belief. Irrespective of caste or creed, there is widespread feeling that God is the teacher and helper of humanity. Deeper is the feeling that One exists who can put right everything that has been spoilt. When one soul prays to that One, there is a desire for help in resolving problems. If God had really created everything, then my woes would also be His will – and we know that cannot be the case.

Further stages in meditation

Meditation involves the consideration of the above points. God is the source of all our needs and is the essence of all relationships. The mind is disconnected from the five power-consuming engines of sight, sound, taste, touch and smell by means of deep reflection: 'I am a soul… a point of light…' After taking the first three steps outlined at the end of Chapter 2, the soul is connected to the powerhouse of spiritual energy, God. In that one tiny star of conscient light that is God, there is such an unlimited quantity of virtues and power, and I am His child. Love is diverted from human beings and physical possessions towards God. Using my mind and intellect for this highest purpose I consciously direct the mind and intellect towards fulfilling this relationship with God.

Meditation is not like prayer in which we have no clear concept of what happens to our prayers or to whom we are praying. It visualises a meeting between the soul and the Supreme Soul. The following table compares the characteristics of human souls with those of the Supreme Soul.

Human Souls	Supreme Soul
They take human bodies and experience birth, life and death.	Never comes into the cycle of birth and death.
They are subject to change and the dualities of pleasure and pain, growth and decay, happiness and sorrow.	Changeless. The one beyond dualities.
They remember and forget their nature.	God is the ocean of knowledge.
They are seekers of peace and happiness.	God is the one being sought. He is the bestower of peace and happiness.
They lose their power and become weak.	God is the constant and external source of all spiritual power.
They are brothers.	God is the father and mother.
They come into, greed, lust and attachment.	God is bondageless, the liberator of all, including the sages, saints, holy teachers and gurus.
They become worshippers.	God is ever worship-worthy.
They have desires based on bodily needs, name and fame.	God is completely desireless and selfless.
They have physical bodies.	God's form is incorporeal.
They cannot liberate humanity.	God is the uplifter of all.
They become impure through body-consciousness.	God is the purifier.
They are caught up by the present, have distorted knowledge of the past and no accurate knowledge of the future.	God is the knower of the three aspects of time.
They are takers.	God is the giver; He takes nothing.

Meditation exercises

Remembering the Supreme Soul

I am in front of the Father of the soul... I feel myself being drawn like a needle toward a magnet... As I come closer, I realise who it is that I am in front of... I recognise my Supreme Father,... a blissfully radiant orb of pure and unlimited love... a starlike entity like myself but with unlimited power... I picture this meeting... I, the soul, am meeting the Supreme Soul,... the ocean of love,... the ocean of peace,... the ocean of knowledge,... radiating so much power... I, the soul, am in union with the One whom I have been seeking for so many births... How lucky I am to be able to come here to absorb all the qualities and powers of the Supreme Soul... Like a sponge, I soak up so much love... I fill up with peace,... overflow with joy... I think about who it is... I am now with the Supreme Soul... My fortune is so great... Waves from this ocean of love break on the shore of my mind... unlimited peace... All burdens are melting in the fire of this love... I am now stable... with the changeless one... He is not in the physical world... I realise how much time I have wasted looking for the incorporeal in the physical world... You are the source of peace... I am now with You in our home of golden-red light... filling myself with Your perfect qualities.

Remembering my relationship with Him

I now realise my eternal relationship with You... In the physical world I have a physical father... I have had many physical fathers in my journey of many births... but You are my spiritual... highest... eternal Father... You are just here in our sweet home of light,... radiating infinite and unchanging love and peace,... filling my thoughts with understanding... You are my father, my mother,... my teacher,... my guide,... my companion,... everything... and You are just a thought away... We are together here in the world where I dwelt before I took my first birth... How lucky I am to have found You... after so much searching... You fill me full of peace, love, knowledge... You, the Father of fathers... the Teacher of teachers... the Guru of gurus... I am with You.... there is no one between us... I feel all frustration being burnt away in the fire of this pure love... I have finally arrived at my destination... My search for You has ended... Now I only wish to be like You... totally merciful, benevolent... ever-giving.

Chapter 4 *Karma* and *Yoga*

Introduction to the Law of *Karma*

Karma means action. We souls are actors in this unlimited world drama. It is inherent in us to come to this field of action to act and reap the fruits of those actions, to express and to experience. Indeed, life can be summed up by these two words: expression and experience.

The idea that we reap what we sow is as old as philosophy itself. Newton's law of action and reaction is the physical interpretation of the same truth. Whether we consider ourselves religious or not, we always have some notion of good and bad, right and wrong. In every field of human endeavour there is always importance placed on the ethical aspects. We cannot deny that one part of the self is the 'conscience' or that 'small inner voice' which sometimes commands and sometimes protests. Our actions are basically motivated by a desire to be peaceful, comfortable and in balance. No one deliberately wants to be miserable.

History itself attests to the quest of humanity to find an ideal social system, captured in such mottos as 'liberty, equality, fraternity'. Unfortunately, the practical reality mocks these ideals. So, something is wrong. Our knowledge of ourselves and of the laws of action which govern our time here has proven to be totally inadequate. Though we have empirically analysed the world to a high degree, we have totally missed the principles which manage it. Religions and ethical systems are diverse and this in itself has caused many conflicts. The conduct of one system of belief, when imposed on another, has produced much war and bloodshed.

The kaleidoscope of legal systems and social customs only allow a fractured view of the true way to act. When a system which dictates what is right and wrong is imposed on individuals, it suggests that the individuals do not themselves have a natural awareness of right and wrong, of what is beneficial, what is harmonious or what is harmful and so on. One might ask, 'What is an accurate understanding of the correct way to act?' Relative to the state of mind of each individual or group of individuals within a certain culture, society or religion, disagreement and conflict arise in the interminable debate on this question.

What medicine should be given? What form of government should we have? What is the best method of education? Which actions liberate? What is 'sinful'? Which actions lead to God and which lead away from Him? The struggle for answers leads to disunity in the world, and results initially from a fundamental misunderstanding of the law of *karma,* or action, which governs us individually and socially. Why are we here? Why was she born in the gutter? Why was he born in ascendancy to the throne? Why was I born here, he there? Why is she clever and beautiful? Why is he mentally retarded, crippled and blind? Why does the egotistical bully who browbeats his business companions, fiddles his income tax return and beats his wife, attain outstanding worldly success? Why does the timid, quiet little widow who has never said a harsh word to anyone, live in appalling conditions and die unwanted and uncared for? Why did he have to 'die'? Why did he do that to me? Why is there so much suffering? Why this, why that?

The cries of injustice are endless. In fact, at the basis of any mental tension, there is always a 'why', 'what' or 'how'. To be assailed by such questions implies little or no understanding of the 'karmic parameters' which determine each situation. The first aspects we should look at are the dynamics of the soul: how the mind, intellect and *sanskar* work together to produce actions. My actions leave impressions which give rise to thoughts, which affect decisions, which lead to further actions and further impressions. At any moment I am both experiencing the consequence of some past thought-decision-action pattern and also creating future thought-decision-action patterns and therefore situations.

In every situation thoughts based on previous impressions simultaneously arise. I see a snarling dog, and because, in the past, I was bitten by a dog, I remember that I should get away as quickly as possible. I send a mental direction to my legs and I run my body away. When I understand that every action is motivated by previous experience and every result is the fruit of action, the question why something has occurred is automatically answered. I myself have created all the conditions in which I find myself.

This necessarily takes into account the fact of reincarnation. It is the only answer to the vastly different conditions souls experience at the time of birth: different bodies, sexes, parents, societies, levels of wealth, levels of health. At this very moment each one of us is living amid the consequences of every thought and action we have ever performed. My state of mind, social position, profession, relations, connections, everything that surrounds me is pulling at me or pushing me. This truth has to be understood thoroughly. In the apparent chaos there is absolute order; there are no 'accidents'.

Further, if I experience sorrow, it is I who have caused it. My past thoughts and decisions have been inadequate in facing things. This has created a state of mind susceptible to sorrow. It is my weakness and I alone can repair it. It requires effort, but this is the very law of *karma:* every effort brings a result. If I experience sorrow, it is self-abuse. The more pain I cause myself, the more I desire to be free from it, but ironically the experience of this pain often results in my performing further bad actions. These in turn bring further pain. It is not difficult to see how it has come about that much of the suffering in the world is on the mental level.

In continuing negativity, I am strengthening the attitude and experience that produce sorrow, my will power, or strength of intellect, is further weakened and the control of my 'self' is further out of my grasp. Peace continues to diminish.

It is inevitable that interaction between individuals, based on weak, unreasoned and wrong attitudes, takes place and this causes further complications. Not only does the soul lack faith in itself, but it views others with doubt, suspicion, cynicism or annoyance. This describes the body-conscious state internally and socially.

When I act towards another under the influence of body-consciousness, the other is harmed slightly or greatly, either immediately or after some time. For example, harsh words are spoken which pierce another's heart as truly as an arrow. At some future time I must experience the result of this; as surely as if I throw a ball up into the air it will come back to me with the same force, whether immediately, after some minutes, months, years or even after some births. The fruits, both bitter and sweet, that grow from the seeds that I plant have to be eaten by me. It is not necessary to go into the 'whys' and 'wherefores' of every action. It is just necessary to accept personal responsibility for the state of one's life.

The yogi in action

By definition, a Raja Yogi is one who has a mental link with the Supreme Soul, the source of all goodness. This, coupled with an understanding of the laws of action which govern the behaviour of souls, means that one does not have to renounce society in order to achieve enlightenment. Rather, the soul filled with illumination faces society directly, with understanding and the compassion to serve it and to elevate it so that it becomes pure once again.

The soul becomes elevated, not by the renunciation of responsibilities or worldly duties, but by a renunciation of the negativity that exists within the role being played. The Raja Yogi does not try to escape social obligations but rather purifies them through becoming filled with light, love, peace and happiness. This stage of self-awareness and God-communication imparts a subtle richness into one's life pattern.

There are those who believe that the elevated state is beyond society and its trimmings. They find a quiet spot in the jungle or a monastery and contemplate deeper things. There are others who are stuck in the quicksand of their problems and believe society's renunciates to be saints. However, holiness and virtue are qualities attained in one's life situation, not in running away from it. The Raja Yogi understands that the elevated state is not merely a matter of elevated thoughts, but elevated actions for the benefit of the self and the world. We are what we do and not so much what we imagine ourselves to be. The external circumstances are merely the unfolding of what we are internally.

Spiritual vision or 'drishti'

In a state of high self-regard, the awareness of oneself as a spiritual being performing pure action brings the awareness that other beings are also souls performing through their bodies. When there is this *drishti* this way of seeing another person as a spiritual being, when the attitude of soul-to-soul is maintained, then there is true communication and pure interaction and the desired state of peace, happiness and purity occurs automatically. If you achieve a state in which you are naturally peaceful, pure and happy, you can be sitting anywhere and, because the thought vibrations emanating from you, the soul, are of such high quality, other beings are necessarily being served by you.

The loss of perspective

The forces which interact to produce the phenomena of world history and geography: souls, matter and God, are threaded by the law of *karma*. When there is mental communion with God, the soul's relationship with matter changes. This means that the internal love-link that the soul has with the Supreme is reflected in the performance of the soul in the material world and in the degree to which the soul has mastery over matter: firstly over the senses of the body and through that, over the colours, shapes and sounds of the material world.

We have continually sought to understand which way to act, but have lost our sense of direction for various reasons:

We forgot that we were soul-actors.
We became lost on the stage.
We became over-identified with our costume, the physical bodies.
We lost sight of the story of the drama.
We forgot that we were residents of the soul world.
Owing to body-consciousness, the soul severed its subtle connection with the Supreme Soul.

What is *karma*? – deeper meanings

Karma is the activity of the soul through the body – thinking, breathing, seeing, touching and moving are *karmas*. These take place according to the law of *karma*: for every action there is an equal and opposite reaction. The types of action which we do reflect our inner state, and form our 'character'. Since we are responsible for our actions, we have to consider their effects on others and ourselves. Even our thoughts affect and create the surrounding atmosphere.

Self-realisation and *karma*

Self-realisation is the recognition and understanding of the soul's actions and reactions. Unless we have a deep concern for this, we cannot progress. We must see if an action is beneficial and channelled into the service of others for then it is of service to the self. If we do happen to perform some harmful action, our knowledge and yoga will give the power to change, and to realise 'past is past'.

The cycle of actions

When the soul is on the field of action, the process of mind-intellect-*sanskaras* begins to spin as the role manifests. According to the amount of control the intellect exercises over the *sanskaras*, the soul can either fly up into the heights of happiness or plunge into the depths of depression. When the soul is reminded of its original state, it automatically starts to spin in a positive direction. When the soul plummets into the tangle of matter and action, it spins in a negative direction. The soul has within itself latent bondages to matter and also the potential to soar into liberation.

Why practise Raja Yoga?

Unless the soul regains its original attributes of purity, peace and bliss, it cannot escape suffering and grief. Purity is the foundation of peace and prosperity. For purity the soul requires absolution and the removal of every trace of negativity. Souls are burdened with the accumulated negative *sanskaras* of their previous births, the extent of which varies from soul to soul. According to the law of *karma*, the soul has to experience suffering as a punishment for its wrongful acts or 'sins'.

A pure soul does not suffer. The evidence that most human beings are bearing grief and suffering in some form shows that nowadays souls are carrying a load of negative *sanskaras,* resulting from 'sins' committed in this and their past lives. A question can be asked: 'Can a soul be relieved of all its past sins through suffering for the same in its present life?' Not really because, owing to the cyclic nature of the thought process, there is a cumulative effect of negative *sanskaras* which forces the soul to perform more negative actions than it can clear through suffering. That is why the degrees of purity of the soul decrease continuously. The downfall becomes steeper owing to the cumulative effect of vices. Negative *sanskaras* give rise to negative thoughts which lead to negative actions, resulting in the formation of still more negative *sanskaras.* Thus, souls are caught in a downward spiral from which they are unable to release themselves.

Raja Yoga, however, opens the door to God and, through rising above all physical laws, the effects of sins can be absolved. Through connection with the purest, the Supreme Soul, the soul is automatically purified and moves further towards its original state of purity and bliss.

Meditation exercises

Purifying the sanskaras

Stay in this meditation for ten minutes, creating your own thoughts based on : *I am a tiny seed,… the seed of all my births…I am now radiant in my original state…in front of my Supreme Father filling with His power…I feel that His light is purifying me,… transforming me.*

The clearing of 'sin'

The belief that we have inherited sin from the time of Adam is not true. Each soul has become impure by its own actions during its births. We ourselves became impure and peaceless through losing our self-awareness; so it is useless to blame anyone else. The soul itself has coloured the changing circumstances with its own state of mind and changing fortunes.

It is too easy to blame 'so-and-so'. Today, everyone blames someone else: 'It's the capitalists', 'It's the religions', 'It's the establishment', 'It's the social pressures', 'It's the devil', 'It's my wife', 'It's my boss'. Few can see that their own unhappiness is because of their own weakness. The 'devil' is just a symbolic personification of these negative forces at work in every soul.

The soul itself creates its accounts, good and bad. So the soul itself must balance them. No human soul, whether Christ or Buddha or even some guru or spiritual guide, can settle someone else's account of sins. In this respect many souls are being misled by those who claim to be able to alter or interfere with the workings of the laws of *karma*. The ones claiming this have their own accounts of 'sins' to settle. While they still remain in a physical body, they are within the bounds of the same laws that apply to all. The law of *karma*, of reaping and sowing, applies to the individual and yet, of course, is social in its implications.

The account of impure actions can only be balanced by pure actions on the part of the 'doer', the soul. Truly pure actions can only be performed when one is in a state of soul-consciousness and in remembrance of the one beyond action, the Supreme Soul. In burning love for God sins can be rapidly incinerated. To this end the soul needs only to increase its love for God. Blind faith, penance, worship or despair will not help.

Becoming free of bondages

The bondages that tie me to people or things, or that tie me up inside in the form of negative attitudes or emotions, reveal the extent to which I am still in the grip of my past. So, what do I have to do to become free? The way out from the 'jungle of thorns', created by my past, to the 'garden of flowers', is embodied in the following steps:
1. Acceptance of personal responsibility.
2. Recognition of the difference between the *sanskaras* that will take me toward my original state and help me maintain soul- and

God-consciousness and those that take me into the trap of body-consciousness and negative action.
3. Decision to stop forthwith the development of body-conscious *sanskaras* by paying attention to thoughts. If I can kill body-consciousness even in thoughts, it will lose its power totally.
4. Elimination of uncleared, negative karmic accounts, manifest in my *sanskaras*, through deep communion with the Supreme Soul.
5. Accrual of credit through pure and God-inspired actions for the spiritual welfare of others.

Usually there is a huge chasm between our inner illuminations and our outer material life. Our thoughts may follow a spiritual orientation, while our actions still trail the path of accustomed mistakes and imperfect influences.

The soul, through many, many experiences, has become a creature of habit, almost completely at the mercy of its own negativity. Many of our lives have become a repetition of the same theme, giving an illusion of novelty through different bodies, families, places of birth, cultures, skin colour and sex, but always repeating the same mistakes. The soul identifies itself with the body and becomes engulfed in that role, lost in an exhausting whirlwind of scenes which produce a torrent of thoughts and a short-sighted intellect.

In the attempt to halt the deafening rush of the *sanskara*-thought-decision-action-*sanskara* process, the soul invents the most marvellous mental recipes of escapes. The intellect busies itself as the strategist, through a special relationship, through sensual experience, through drugs, music, sex and so on, but ultimately it forfeits itself to negative *sanskaras*, which grow stronger and stronger. So what are we to do?

Instead of turning to the old sources outside and around us, I must learn to go into the experience of soul-consciousness and, through that, go to the ultimate source, Shiva. I must learn to practise remembrance of Him in the situations that are most difficult: in the street, on the bus, in the madness of rushing to work or in looking after the children.

I should not leave the contemplation and practice of spirituality for quiet moments only. After all, I am only one person, not two. I cannot lead a separate spiritual life from a worldly life and hope to progress. To say that there isn't time to practise these things conveys that there is no control over the external life. Those practising Raja Yoga execute their daily responsibilities accurately. For them, the least circumstance becomes an occasion for victory, an opportunity to accumulate spiritual credit for the future. The soul has an aim, a real orientation and assurance of going somewhere instead of nowhere and this really incites the force of change.

One by one, mental constructions and thought bondages are eliminated and there is just no need to daydream about methods of escape. In daily life in the midst of a number of occupations, the soul can replenish itself. It becomes clear that the goal of life is in life, on this earth, with the feet planted squarely on the ground and not a 'pseudo-truth' that keeps the head in the clouds. True spirituality is gauged by our actions and not by our metaphors.

> *Thought ropes which tie me down,*
> *Keep me on the ground*
> *In the net of sound;*
> *Break these fetters of mental illusion.*

Personal experience of the author

When I first started to feel my total responsibility for all the aspects of my life, it seemed too heavy a weight to bear. How convenient it was to lay the blame outside myself for any difficult situation or emotional or physical pain. However, the challenge that I could rebuild the future of my choice was so intriguing that, to take the rudder of my life, to leave the bondages created in the past and sail smoothly into a brilliant future, seemed no less than a natural duty to myself, to God and to the world around me. After all, absorbing as much benefit as I could from each passing scene would eliminate the negative impressions of unbeneficial acts, and would help me enjoy an obstacle-free present and would be tracing a clear, certain and fear-free future.

Moreover, I would be able to maintain such a positive vibration that others around me would also be inspired. Through this understanding a new panorama of possibilities unfolded before me and I started to follow, in depth, the philosophy of *karma* with the view that emotional and spiritual freedom is my birthright.

Karma Yoga

Raja Yoga contains within it *karma yoga* also. *Karma yoga* implies two things:
- *yoga* by which the *karmas* are elevated and purified;
- those *karmas* by which the remembrance of God is maintained and strengthened.

As was stated, *yoga*, the loving remembrance of God, is not just a 'sitting' matter. If we approach meditation from this angle, any real change in practical life takes a very long time. We should not only use meditation to improve our actions, but also modify our actions to improve our meditation. In this way, theory and practice should be simultaneous. As the soul takes from the Supreme Soul, it gives to the world, thus increasing the capacity to take and give.

In the sitting meditation, be it five minutes or two hours, the soul dives deeply into itself and establishes an unbroken mental link with the Supreme. When the 'sitting' finishes and the soul has to go back into the world of action and responsibility, the link need not be forgotten. The hands can be involved with the work and the mind can still be with the Supreme Soul.

Practical aids to maintain yoga while performing actions

1. The seeds, the inspirations planted in sitting meditation, should be carried into action. Powerful thoughts carried straight away into action always yield powerful results.
2. The remembrance should be that the soul is the child and student of God and should reflect that father and teacher through its actions.
3. The remembrance of God as a constant companion sustains an internal relationship with Him while performing actions.
4. Churn over points of knowledge by relating them to your immediate terms of reference. For example, when washing clothes we can think of how *yoga* washes the soul free from the stains of matter.
5. Practise going beyond sound in one second. At different times during the day, stop, pack up all worldly thoughts and spend a few minutes in silent communion. This is a really powerful way to strengthen the intellect. After a few minutes return to the world of sound with the reinforced awareness of being an actor.
6. Practise seeing all those who come into contact with you as souls, tiny points of light. In this way the soul will not be pulled into body-consciousness and will avoid negative interaction.

Karma and reincarnation

Human life is based on interrelationships. These, in turn, are based on the different *sanskaras*. They determine the course of life, the nature of the soul's activities and its physical placement in a particular environment.

What happens at 'death'?

When the body has become unserviceable because of age or disease, or it suffers a fatal injury, the soul leaves the body. At the moment of death the soul withdraws its energy from the organs of the body and vacates its seat in the middle of the forehead. Like a bird, it leaves the cage made of skin and bone and, taking its *sanskaras,* it enters into another, a new body, in the womb of the new mother. This normally happens between the fourth and fifth month of pregnancy. From the very birth, the *sanskaras* of a soul are apparent whether the 'newborn' baby is happy, unbothered, sad, shy, mischievous, quiet, violent or agitated.

Death occurs at the precise moment when the account of giving and taking with other souls through a particular body is finished. The new birth is determined by the soul's account with another set of souls. One may be born into a cultured, wealthy family, another as a beggar; one may be born deaf, dumb, blind or crippled, another with a strong supple body. The type of body and the conditions of birth are determined by both the thoughts and actions performed previously and by the accumulated account of giving and taking with other souls. The preconditions of the new birth, the when, where, how and why, lie merged in the soul. The leaving of one body and the taking of another are nearly always confusing and soon the details of the old life are obliterated by the new. Just in one day we forget so much. After having slept for a while, after some injury or shock, or even after a change in place, company or circumstances, many things are forgotten. Death of the body is a great shock to the soul, especially if there was great attachment to that body. The new set of circumstances in the new body is bewildering. Since the body and brain are not developed, the soul cannot express its memory and so it laughs and cries when it cannot recognise anyone, or when it wishes to express itself. By the time the body is developed, the soul has forgotten and has become accustomed to the new conditions and the new parents. The predominant *sanskaras,* developed in past lives, soon begin to manifest themselves with new details.

Instinct explained by rebirth

Every baby has some tendency or another from the moment of birth, tendencies formed by past thoughts and actions. The soul doesn't inherit tendencies genetically. All that is transferred genetically is the physical appearance, the colour of eyes, shape of nose and so on. There is a certain amount of influence acquired from the new situation, as in the saying: 'He has his father's bad temper.' The fact that the soul was born into that family to pay off its accounts one way or the other indicates that the soul has performed similar actions in a previous birth. That someone has a fear of heights, someone else a fear of being enclosed, indicates that they suffered from similar experiences in a previous birth. The soul's desire for peace and happiness may be termed 'instinctive' but is certainly not biological.

Karmic accounts from previous births

Many times one meets someone with the feeling of either attraction or repulsion and the thought: 'Where have I seen this person before?' What happens is that the soul recognises the other soul, even though their bodies are different from the last time they met. Someone may be a source of comfort or inspiration, while another, for no apparent cause, elicits a feeling of indignation: 'Why does he treat me like this; I have never done anything to him?'

There are some who, even at a young age, achieve extraordinary proficiency in some branch of knowledge, art or music, while others, in spite of their best efforts, achieve nothing. Identical twins may be born to the same parents and have the same environment, food and education, but all their lives, their nature and 'fortunes' will be completely different. All these examples can only be explained by the law of cause and effect over a series of births.

Important points about reincarnation

1. The human soul does not transmigrate into animal species, just as an apple seed does not grow into an orange tree. The human soul always takes a human body.
2. The soul is distinct from any of the bodies it adopts.
3. The world's population is increasing at such a rapid rate, indicating that the souls already here are taking rebirth and also that there are new ones coming down continuously from the soul world.
4. The cycle of action and reaction is never-ending. The soul must continue to play its entire role until all actions have played out their results. This may require more than one body.
5. The lives of a soul are like serialised installments of a novel in a magazine.
6. If one believed that one has to reap the fruit of one's actions, if not in

this birth, but in another one, a person would surely feel less inclined to perform negative actions.

7. Without reincarnation it is impossible to explain how every soul has reached its present peaceless state. The cumulative effect of the vices weighs heavily on the soul and causes it unhappiness in the present. It is precisely this burden from which the Supreme Soul can relieve us. The end of the present cycle of birth and rebirth is approaching its conclusion.

All life's questions explained by the karmic process

However difficult or painful the situation is in which I find myself, I have put myself there by my previous choices. I am not the victim of some angry or vengeful God. I am the victim of a past I created myself. When I appear in a new body, for example, I do not start from scratch but I pick up exactly where I have left off in the previous birth. If, for example, in one birth I had a passion for pitching rocks through the proverbial greenhouse, then I am born into the equivalent of a human greenhouse which gets its panes bashed in. I may not be able to see with these gross eyes the effect of all my actions but, with time, there is definitely just retribution. If I cause harm to others during one life, there might be instant mental unrest but, if not, the suffering comes in the form of a sad death or a sad next life. If, in one life, I give generously to build a hospital or place of learning, I am born in the next life with good health or good education.

Vikarma – Sukarma

The soul may be locked away in a prison of negative desires, fears and ambitions. It may be soaring free on the wings of soul-consciousness. The soul creates its own destiny. *Vikarmas* are those actions performed in body-consciousness. *Sukarmas* are those actions performed in soul-and God-consciousness. The table on the previous page gives examples of these kinds of actions.

Personal experience of the author: true charity

I used to think that charity was a matter of helping the poor with handouts, the sick with medicine, the hungry with food, and I would have a sense of guilt seeing them. I used to think the vices were smoking or drinking excessively and that sin was a gross transgression of law – stealing, killing, adultery.

Consciousness in action

Body-consciousness	Yogic consciousness
The soul is influenced by any of the vices, principally anger, greed, ego, lust or attachment.	The soul brings its original qualities of peace, power, purity, love and bliss into action.
The soul is unable to settle its past karmic accounts and so karmic debts accumulate.	The soul balances out its karmic debt and actually begins to store credit.
Relationships become bondages and causes of sorrow rather than enjoyment.	Relationships with others are purified and elevated. There is no sense of bondage.
Conflicts, which can be called 'clashes' of *sanskaras*, occur between souls. There is negativity, sensitivity and disunity.	Souls are able to harmonise with each other with happiness and peace.
Actions cause sorrow and loss for the self and others in contact.	Actions fill the self and others with happiness and peace.
Actions are performed to attract or impress others by the physical identity.	Actions are performed to bring others also into relationship with God.
Charity performed for others has the shadow of ego and has limited results.	The highest charity of introducing other souls to the Supreme Soul is performed through thoughts, words and actions.

But now my view of sin and charity has changed immensely. Helping the poor and needy is of course worthy but I question if I truly am helping them out of their karmic situation? Rather, let me not involve others in physical debt to me. Let me help them come to an understanding of their situation and connect them to the Supreme Father who alone can give them the power to pull them out of their karmic spiral. Now I just wish to fill others, whoever they may be, with the beauty and experience of the soul-conscious state.

After some experience of meditation, I started to see how much can be done for those around me, just by remaining in the stage of 'om shanti'.

Meditation exercise

Serving the world

Just by entering into yogic consciousness, the soul is able to serve the whole world. Physical charity is limited to the physical plane. We can only be in one place at any one time and only with a few others. When the soul enters the consciousness of its original state, it can become a channel for God's qualities to flow to all others. In this state I am instantly in contact with all others because, on this level, there are no physical divisions like distance. My thoughts can reach out and serve all at the same time.

'I am a soul... a tiny star,... like Shiva Baba,... radiating my original qualities... I become so small,... so detached from the name and form of the body... and those associated with that name and form,... just a soul,... so concentrated... I am now in front of the Supreme Father,... Shiva Baba,... receiving,... receiving... and through me, His light is spreading to all souls everywhere...'

Chapter 5 Raja Yoga and the Wheel of Life

> *Down the corridors of time,*
> *I look to find*
> *My perfect state shining just the same.*
> *What I was I will be again.*
> *Beneath the canopy of stars,*
> *We play our roles,*
> *Brothers all, playing in a game.*
> *What we were we will be again.*

The Raja Yogi and time

Self-transformation is inspired when the soul can see its entire part acted out against the backdrop of world history. It is not sufficient to know only the present condition; the soul also needs insight into what has been and what will be.

There exists a unity of principle behind the great variety of phenomena which surrounds us, and in this chapter we will discuss this principle and how it affects us souls. One of the greatest difficulties can thus be overcome: that of relating to this present world, without experiencing fear, frustration or tension. We have seen how body-consciousness severely limits our view of things, concealing the reasons behind happenings. We can only see the abundant paradoxes without understanding them. Religion seems relegated to the mere performance of sets of rituals while science endeavours to create an artificial paradise. Little do we realise that, without a strong and pure character, all the luxury and the false sense of well-being it provides can only give fleeting happiness, interwoven with fits of depression. So, what is this world? Is there any plan or purpose? What is the principle to which the flow of events is tied?

World history is a drama

The interplay between souls, nature and God is what constitutes the cycle of world history. We shall call it the world drama. God is the director, the souls are the actors and nature is the stage.

The drama is the story of human souls, their rise and fall, victory and defeat, happiness and suffering, knowledge and ignorance, liberation and bondage. It is the story of the play of good and evil forces and of the different stages through which the souls pass in five different epochs. It is a story of how the souls mistakenly identify themselves with their perishable bodies and how this leads to a decline in all levels of human activity. This decline then reaches its extreme until souls turn again to God and restore their true identities and regain their former spiritual heights. Decline, consequences of the law of cause and effect, the emergence of vices, the increase in worship, the advent of pure souls as founders of religions, the emergence of many religions, the growth of fanaticism and confusion, war and disease, and finally the liberation of souls from their self-created bondages – these are the salient features of the drama.

Just as in an ordinary drama, an actor, wearing a suitable costume, acts out his part at a predetermined moment, so in this world drama, the soul-actors perform their roles, each at their assigned 'cue'. This role lies dormant in the soul in the form of impressions, until the right time period triggers the qualities inherent in the soul and it makes its appearance on the stage.

Those impressions become thoughts, which are then translated into words or actions. The total role of every individual exists in latent form within the soul while the soul is in the soul world. When the soul appears in the physical world, that role begins to manifest itself. The soul begins to act and after the accumulation of birth upon birth of action, it eventually becomes trapped in their consequences. It forgets its own origin and is, instead, bound by various identities, objects, ideologies and relationships and starts to search for a way out of them.

The world drama, or world history, is but the collective play of all the individual parts of the soul-actors. The soul awaits in the soul world, 'backstage', until the situation is conducive for it to enter the drama. Once each soul is here, it must remain until all souls have come onto the stage. At that time there is major transformation and all souls, except for a few, return home to the soul world. And the drama begins again. The only possible way that life can thus eternally continue is if time is cyclic.

The cycle of time

In recorded history, time has always been an enigma. To some, time is merely a regulator. Everything they have to do is divided into hours, minutes and seconds. In the modern world it is normal to be slaves to time. To others, time is seen as a continuous subtle thread to which all events and scenes are tied. Whichever, time stands as the measure of processes. Though time is not tangible, it can be understood. The nature of time can be described by the processes which it measures or, in other words, the processes which take place within time.

Human beings thought that the earth was flat until it was discovered that one could travel in a straight direction for a certain distance and arrive back at the same point. So after the invention of the telescope and the voyages of the great navigators we had to change our understanding of the world and, in this way, all subsequent scientific theories have continued to change and become more refined. Through the 'apparatus' of meditation and spiritual knowledge we penetrate new dimensions and come to a cyclic understanding of time.

One theory that scientists have postulated is that this is an expanding universe in which originally all matter was densely concentrated and there was a great explosion, since which time all matter has been expanding outward. This is called the 'big bang' theory. One thing this theory overlooks, however, is the most basic of all cosmic principles: the law of cause and effect. What was the cause of this 'bang'?

On the other hand, most would agree that time and space are infinite. Even the symbol for infinity, the figure eight written sideways, suggests something that has no beginning or end. One can safely say that the law of cause and effect operates forever. Each point in the cyclic flow of events gives cause to the next point, until eventually it arrives at the same point that it begins from. Time as a cycle is the only possible way that we can bring infinity and the law of cause and effect together and tie them neatly into one 'unified field'.

What does cyclic time imply?

The most important point of all is that if time is cyclic, there can be no beginning nor end to anything else, because everything exists in the physical universe with time. Everything is eternal and can be measured in terms of space-time co-ordinates.

If there were a creation *ex-nihilo* (from nothing), then we are left with the difficulty of trying to explain how God was created. As it is reasonable to accept that there was no beginning to God, it is just as reasonable to accept that souls and matter had no beginning. With a cyclic view of time we need not lose time in the dilemma of creation theories but see the universe as it is: a complexity of energies, physical and metaphysical, that both expand and contract, that can neither be created nor destroyed and which are bound by the laws of cause and effect to a never-beginning and never-ending swirl of change. The processes of integration and disintegration of forms and events never cease but the components that come together to make up those forms and events, atoms and souls, while retaining their intrinsic 'individualness' merely pass through a series of changes of position and function.

Cyclic time implies that God neither creates matter nor souls, but all three 'forces' co-exist and interact eternally to produce all phenomena.

Energy and entropy

The first law of thermodynamics shows us that energy can neither be created nor destroyed. The implications of this are considerable, especially if one considers that everything is energy. Matter itself is a form of condensed energy (as discussed in Chapter 1). The second law shows us that wherever there is movement, energy at a higher level is transformed into energy at a lower level. For example, in burning coal to run a steam engine we are merely transforming potential energy into kinetic: as the coal burns, it loses its potential and the energy is dissipated in churning the pistons of the engine. Some of the energy is lost through gases, some through heat and so on. In time the amount of energy expended by the coal becomes less and so more coal is needed.

This law is also called the law of entropy, which states that, with time, energy which is going from a potential state to a kinetic state diminishes until there is nothing left. A fire burns out, the body grows up, gets old and 'dies', a bouncing ball comes to a stop – all these are examples of entropy. In dissipating energy from a purely potential state to its kinetic state, entropy also implies a progression from an ordered to a chaotic state. For example, the first bounces of a ball are strong and ordered, even predictable; its last bounces are 'all over the place'. A youthful body is strong and disease-free; an old body is wracked with complications. The human souls also start off their individual journeys of birth and rebirth at their highest stages and move through history to a state of weakness and disorder in the same way that batteries discharge their energy through use. Putting these two laws together in view of cyclic time, we come to some interesting implications:

- The cycle is a closed system in which everything has always existed and will continue to exist. There are no additions or subtractions, no new matter or souls created. There are a fixed number of both.

- Within the cycle of time the total entropy is continually increasing. That means that the initial strength or potential of souls and nature is continually being used up through movement and action. But the time comes when the energy lost has to be 'topped up' again, otherwise everything would get weaker and weaker forever.
- If we take the 'start' of the cycle of history as the moment in which there is the highest potential in all things, nature and souls, then the 'end' of the cycle must be the period in which that potential is being 'topped up' or 'recreated'.
- The only 'force' left to carry this out is God, the only being who never loses His intrinsic energy, who never passes through the process of entropy, who is forever 'almighty'.

The analogy of the water cycle

All the cycles of nature go from high potential to low energy and back again: for example, the water cycle. Rain water falls, according to gravity, and through river systems continues towards the sea, becoming more and more sluggish as it goes. The sun (the external 'force' in this case) shines on the water and it returns to its potential state in the clouds from where it falls again and the cycle is repeated.

The water cycle is helpful in understanding the rise, fall and the rise again of human souls. From the clouds, drops of pure water fall on top of a mountain, joining together and becoming a stream, dancing happily over the rocks. They are pure at this stage, but not entirely free, because they are bound to completing a downward journey towards the sea. That journey courses through many different types of countryside.

As the 'population' of drops increases, the stream grows in size. Bubbling through the rocks, it picks up impurities in the form of dissolved salts, and the stream becomes a small brownish river, now no longer dancing happily, but moving sluggishly. As it continues, it grows further in size and becomes slower and heavier. It moves past small towns which pour all their waste and effluent into the river and then finally runs through the big cities where all types of chemicals and pollutants join the flow indiscriminately. The river at this stage is totally unrecognisable compared to the beginning of its journey. The original drops are still there, as are the drops that have joined in the journey along the way. The water is no longer pure but full of dissolved salts and mud in colloidal suspension.

The river finally arrives at the ocean. Fortunately, within this cyclic system the drops are 'liberated' by means of evaporation. They 'fly upwards', forming clouds, leaving the impurities behind in the ocean. From the clouds, the drops of pure water fall again on a mountain and the cycle repeats. As in all cyclic processes there is a birth, growth, decline, death and then rebirth.

The 'river' of humanity flows in a similar manner. The souls are like the drops arriving from the soul world, each in its purest state. They adopt bodies. In the first part of the river of history, the population is small, unified and pure. They pass through many births, acquiring the 'salts' of impurities through contact with and influence of the material world. The 'sweet' water becomes 'brackish' and then 'salty'.

The souls become unrecognisable compared to their original state. The only possibility of their being liberated from their acquired impurities is through the influence of God, the 'sun' of knowledge. When the 'river' of humanity has poured itself into an 'ocean of vices', when impurities in the fabric of all human affairs reach their most critical point, God, the Supreme Being, acts to renew the system. The souls are purified, go back to the 'clouds' – in this case – the soul world and come to earth again to go through a new cycle.

We cannot judge the history of humanity on the basis of limited and comparatively recent past facts and figures. This would be like trying to deduct the whole story of a river on the basis of that tiny part of it passing in front. Any particular section of the river may not seem perfect but the whole process is one of perfection. So too with the history of human souls. There is a pure stage and an impure stage, a happy stage, a sad stage, an enlightened stage and an ignorant stage, a day of history and a night of history, a heaven and a hell. There is also the means by which the impure souls can become pure again.

The cycle of birth and rebirth

At first we rest in the unmanifest state as points of light energy. We adopt a human form according to our *sanskaras* (qualities or predispositions). We act out a role on the world stage. This role may be of one birth or it may be of many. Each birth is determined by *sanskaras*. For example, a soldier who dies on the battlefield is likely to be reborn amid military surroundings. The soul goes through this cycle, performing actions which consolidate as *sanskaras* and which, at any point in time, are determining the future situation of the soul (as seen in the previous chapter).

Looking for the causes underlying each birth leads us back to the time when we first descended from the soul world. But even our first birth in the cycle has a cause. It is due to whatever inclinations we had at the end of the previous one. At the end of each cycle we are emancipated from the bondage of negative actions by God, the supreme liberator. Our individual role persists but in a latent form. Our inclinations or *sanskaras* are our eternal bearings. We can never be anyone except ourselves but we oscillate within the limits of that self, between our purest and impurest stages during the cycle of time.

Evolution, creation *ex nihilo* or ...

Perhaps one of the greatest dividers of opinion in the last one hundred years has been the wide acceptance of the theory of evolution. In pondering existence, there have been many opinions offered, but the two most conflicting opinions are either that matter and all life forms were created at once, from nothing, by an almighty God; or that life arose from non-living matter.

We know that everything that exists has always existed. There is no such thing as new creation. Secondly, the ancestors of human beings have always been human beings and not monkeys. The parents of our bodies are human beings, their parents were human beings and so on. Never will we find that some human beings had monkeys for parents nor will we find that human beings emerged from the 'dust'.

Science has demonstrated that all physical things are built of molecules which are based on chemical elements of certain types. These basic elements, which are the building blocks of matter, cannot be simplified by change or by natural chemical processes. All molecules result from a tendency towards neutralisation. Living things are based mainly on different combinations of organic compounds and there is no instance of an inorganic compound evolving into an organic one. What this means is that life has already to be existing before organic compounds can be formed.

Contrary to these simple facts of chemistry, we are asked to believe that, not only did organic compounds evolve from inorganic ones, but that those compounds became living cells and those living cells eventually became a person. Even the simplest cell is as complicated as a city. The gap between the inanimate and the animate is enormous and cannot be bridged even in the most sophisticated laboratories. So there is absolutely no proof for even this first step of the theory of evolution.

Though evolutionary theories have been modified to reflect changing attitudes, we still have a vast amount of literature based on an incredibly tiny amount of circumstantial evidence. Even Darwin himself said: 'To suppose that the eye could have been formed from natural selection seems, I freely confess, to be absurd in the highest degree.' He also said: 'Those who believe that the geological record is in any degree perfect will undoubtedly reject the theory.'

Another unchangeable law is that of biogenesis which states that all life derives from preceding life. All forms of plants and animals have reproduced, are reproducing and will reproduce only their own forms or bodies. This can only be so if time is cyclic and things are eternal.

Irrespective of these cenotaphic laws, the basic defect in the theory of evolution is that it does not take into account the different entities of soul and body. It betrays complete ignorance about the existence of the soul and thus, merely on the basis of gross physical resemblance between the body of people and apes, the latter have been declared to be our ancestors.

The theory of evolution is totally materialistic and its main difficulty still remains: to explain how consciousness is derived from matter. It is just not possible to reconcile the existence of souls with the theory of biological evolution.

The five ages of humanity

The wheel of creation spins endlessly, without pause, transcending the bounds of birth and death. The changes within all souls are reflected in changes in the phenomena of the material world. We are not only traversing our own orbits, but our actions are tied to the actions of others as well. The net effect of these individual and collective actions is the cyclic movement of human history.

The story of the world drama

Contrary to popular theory, our ancestors were neither monkeys nor cave dwellers but human beings who had a deep and natural understanding of the world they inhabited. The original population was small, though growing slowly. This period we have termed 'prehistory', simply because written and reliable records of things and events started only about 2500 years ago. The first age in which everything is at its highest level of purity can be called for simplicity's sake, the golden age. That is followed in sequence by the silver, copper and iron ages and ultimately there is a period of transition from old to new, impure to pure, which can be called the confluence age.

Golden age, *Satyuga* – the age of truth

In the 'beginning' each member of society plays exactly that role for which his or her natural qualities are best suited. Some have the qualities to be rulers and others have the qualities to be subjects. It is a 'hierarchical society' based on divine virtues. This means that different roles are based upon intrinsic qualities and not on false notions of grandeur and social inequalities. Because each soul plays the role to which it is best suited no one complains or covets the role of another. Though there are rulers and subjects, there is neither enforced authority nor submissive subordination. The rulers are simply those who have the greatest virtues and natural wisdom.

The system is held together like a perfect, crystal lattice. Everything is at its highest stage of purity and beauty. Concepts such as value, profit and loss, misery, poverty, sorrow and death do not exist. In a society whose members have much more than they need, trade and exchange are carried out mainly for distribution purposes. With such universal prosperity and internal and external harmony, shortage and the misery it entails are unimaginable.

The system of the golden age is not a conscious philosophy in practice, but rather a natural manifestation of a society whose members are in the highest state of natural soul-consciousness. They instinctively feel their realities as souls and not bodies. Being soul-conscious, they are automatically the masters of their sense organs and of their environment.

This picture is not the idealised paradise; it does not pretend a perpetual youth of blissful innocence. It is the peak of human civilisation in every field of human endeavour: teaching, music, government, drama, linguistics, painting and science. Science is such that it comprehends and harnesses the forces that govern this planet without destroying or polluting the environment. It is the purest use of science and technology at its highest level.

Only the best materials are used in the construction of perfect architecture, the best that nature can provide: gold, diamonds, rubies and so on. The world is a garden in which the seasons vary slightly. Art, dance and music are at their most expressive. There are no borders of land, sea or air. The soul is in perfect balance with all others. Everyone enjoys good health. There is no need for laws or law courts. The only law is love.

Actions in the golden age

Let us imagine an innocent child at play in the present time, exploring, curious, even awestruck, as things present themselves to be acted upon, taken up, cherished, put down and so on. It lives in a world of wonder and builds up its stock of experiences which will later be drawn upon in daily routine.

In the golden age actions are somewhat like this but with important differences. The capacity to harm or be harmed is absent. The reservoir of past births or negative *sanskaras,* waiting to break forth into the mind as the child develops into an adult, are not there. There are pure *sanskaras* in action and also pure *sanskaras* in a latent state. There is neither knowledge of evil nor potentiality for it.

Another difference is that the present-day child is simply reacting to external stimuli, and is at their mercy, whereas the soul, acting through the body in the golden age, expresses itself according to the internal stimuli of pure *sanskaras*. According to time, they come into the mind and are simply translated into actions and innocently become merged again. Each individual is manifesting *sanskaras* of purity, peace and happiness and so each action is perfect. The collective result is that there is complete harmony in the social fabric.

There is no question of performing acts of charity, nor acts of sin, because, on the one side, no one needs upliftment or any sort of moral, financial or physical support and, on the other side there is an absolute incapacity to do evil. This type of action is called neutral action or *akarma*; which implies that, between souls, there are no bondages at all. There are no actions that can be motivated by body-conscious desires or illusions, simply because these don't exist. The souls are at full strength and full illumination. No shadow can be cast over souls who are shining so brightly.

Procreation is not motivated by ego ('I want my name and form to continue'), carried out by lust (bodily gratification) or sustained by attachment ('This is my child'). Conception is of a different form, firstly, because the souls are absolute masters of their bodies and environments and secondly, the bodies themselves are perfect and so have some hormonal differences to the bodies we have at present.

The socio-political system of the kingdom of heaven

There are no political philosophies nor persuasions, no social injustices to be righted, nor causes to fight for. The perfect order of a monarchy system of government is counter balanced by universal, brotherly vision. All souls feel others to be like themselves. Even the rulers treat their subjects as their own mothers and fathers would. The rulers need no ministers or advisers because of their inherent wisdom and divinity and, though there are meetings to organise and programmes to attend, there is no concept of the word 'problem' nor the word 'advice'. Though they represent sovereign power, there is never occasion to issue ordinances that the people would feel as any kind of imposition or authoritarianism.

Society runs smoothly because all are in tune with nature and each other. There is no thought of competition. Family life is in perfect unity because relationships are not based on anger, greed, ego, lust or attachment, but on mutual respect and equality. The behaviour and attitude of all are selfless and sharing. It is a 'self-governed' life in which the soul rules the sense organs and can enjoy perfect comradeship. There is one way of life, one language, one tradition. There are no churches, temples, scriptures, gurus and so on. Religion is life; it is the religion of truth in action. Since there is no conflict within, there is no conflict without.

The sovereigns possess all the qualifications for both religion and government. It is not even possible to compare such divine authority with the religious leaders of today, well-versed though they may be in scriptures and rituals, nor with the kings who linger in our memories. They have the 'light' of religion in their lives, that of purity and peace, and so there is natural respect from all. They are not religious leaders in the sense of being 'upholders of doctrine'. Their virtuous example is simply the focal point of the kingdom. They are not emperors in any despotic sense. Their great royalty of character receives universal acceptance. It is not that no one dares challenge their authority. The very idea of 'challenging' does not exist.

A modern socialist would perhaps be horrified at the thought that all law making was in the hands of an emperor and empress with no outside advice whatsoever. But natural law is at work. There is no need for written law, nor all the machinery to enforce it. The law of the kingdom is the example of the action of its divine leaders. It is this example which all follow; it is natural rule in practice. Lakshmi and Narayan are still worshipped as the first emperor and empress of the golden age. Their very names connote perfection: *Laksh* means 'the aim' and *Narayan* means 'the perfect man'. The 'dynasty' of Lakshmi-Narayan lasts eight generations, and is sometimes referred to as the 'sun dynasty'.

Silver Age, Tretayuga – the decline

Inevitably the slow decline of things starts to be noticed. As spring imperceptibly creeps into summer, the golden age paradise becomes a 'semi-paradise', a silver age (*Tretayuga*, the 'three-quarters' age).

Its beginning is marked by the changing of dynasties: from that of Lakshmi and Narayan to that of Rama and Sita which lasts 12 generations; this is remembered as the 'moon dynasty'. The deities (so called for their divine actions) are discharging their original power and qualities through their actions which affects the whole kingdom. Comparing the golden age and silver age is somewhat like comparing the effect of the sun on colours at full-light and its effect at half-light. The colour and beauty of things are still there but their richness is a little dulled.

In the relationship among souls there is still pure love, but the population is increasing, the kingdom is expanding and, for convenience, is divided into principalities. Material resources are therefore being spread more thinly over a wider area to meet a greater demand. The souls who entered this play are gradually becoming attracted to the things of the senses. Material beauty first allures the soul more and more in each successive birth, into the world of the senses and sensual desires. Though there is hardly any negativity or sorrow, the quality of all things is a little less. There is a difference in the degrees of bliss, power, purity and prosperity.

Heaven to hell

'If the world was so perfect why did it have to fall?' 'Why did we leave the "grace" of God and enter "sin"?' These and similar questions have been long debated and many attempts to explain the 'fall of man' and his subsequent 'banishment from paradise' have been made. Adam and Eve, Satan and the fruit from the tree of life are symbolic attempts to describe what, in fact, was just a natural process. Together, the golden and silver ages constitute the period that we know as 'heaven on earth', the 'Garden of Eden' of the Jews and Christians, the 'Garden of Allah' of the Muslims, the *Vaikunth* of the Hindus, the 'Fields of Osiris' of the Egyptians and so on. It is not a place 'up in the sky' nor is 'hell' a fiery pit underground. They are merely periods of history. The idea that heaven is 'up there' and hell 'down there' comes from periods of history when the consciousness of human beings is either 'higher' or 'lower'. The level of intuitive soul-consciousness deteriorates with time and ultimately the point is reached in which souls no longer have sufficient strength to withstand the encroachments of the material world. It is not that matter suddenly acquires power over souls. Souls simply lose their dominance and start to become the slaves of matter; souls go from a unified and integrated existence into disunity, divergence and degradation.

The 'day' of history becomes 'night'. The river of humanity reaches its first intrusions of brackishness. Now, an insatiable 'lack' gradually begins to motivate actions. The internal 'vacuum' created by loss of the soul's original power starts to 'suck in' influences from the external world. Because the knowledge that souls had in the golden and silver ages was not conscious but intuitive, there is no way of knowing what is happening nor why. This loss of self-awareness is compensated for by material gain. Souls lose the ability to govern themselves and maintain the subtle balance with nature. The fine and beautiful 'crystal lattice' of souls in harmony with nature can no longer be held together naturally and automatically.

Though the process is gradual, the point at which souls lose their self-control can be called the 'breaking-point'. When the subtle forces that have held souls and nature in a mutually beneficial working relationship are suddenly no longer there, the crystal shatters and there is upheaval; earthquakes and natural calamities make the internal confusion in the souls even worse.

The first inklings of desire make themselves more strongly felt; a feeling that the qualities the soul has lost may be gained from others around. There is uneasiness due to the loss of self-certainty and of their environment. The same subtlety that allowed the deities to live in perfect health and enjoy a natural technology of the highest order is now forfeited. They are at the mercy of the elements.

The 'breaking up' of paradise is a recurring theme in the world's mythologies. The civilisation of Atlantis sinks, that is, the consciousness of these previously divine beings 'sinks'. The sun and moon dynasties that were centred on the Indian subcontinent start to spread out. Amid this turmoil of matter and souls, 'hell' is born.

> *The days of gold rolled along,*
> *Unceasing ecstasy,*
> *A kingdom of kindness freshly feeling.*
> *The dawn of all,*
> *The day of understanding.*
> *Nature kissed the harmony*

Within the soul,
Responding gently to the vibrations of peace.
The wheel of time turning slowly,
Spring unfolded into summer.
Still the beauty but some of the magic vanished.
No longer new,
Quality of souls and nature
Faded slightly,
Time devouring the exuberance
Of the players,
Changing bodies like garments
To appear on stage again,
But each time more attracted
To the senses and their desires.
Halfway point!
Awareness lost, confusion.
The elements of nature ceased
To sing their gentle song
And entered into paroxysms of change:
Paradise buried in oblivion.

Copper age, *Dwapuryuga* – the age of duality

This age is the beginning of recorded history. The virtuous state, or the ability to perform truthfully, has been lost and that missing gap has to be filled in. Thus the search to gain back the lost paradise begins, though it is truly 'lost'. The elements of nature combine to produce changes of catastrophic proportions, so much so that even the buildings are buried to such a depth that architectural traces are only now being discovered. The ways and acts of the deities, however, are remembered and they become the figures of our myths and legends, devotion and worship.

The original race is scattered over the face of the earth. Some of these 'pockets of civilisation' become isolated and, in such hostile conditions, rapidly degenerate, forming 'primitive' or 'tribal' societies. Large groups of immigrants from India emerge in Egypt, Sumeria and Babylon, still carrying remnants of the most elevated culture and technology the world has ever known. However, unable to meet the challenges offered by the harsher conditions, they too experience rapid decline. We find a preoccupation in the mythologies of all the major, ancient civilisations about a 'lost paradise' and the beautiful 'gods and goddesses' who ruled there. Pantheism proves that our ancient civilisations are descended from the original deity civilisation.

Ideologies emerge in an effort to rationalise and reverse the fall that is occurring, but no one has sufficient power to bring the tatters of humanity back together. Such attempts have instead served to separate various cultures even more.

Abraham, in approximately 500 BC, creates a religion based on the law of God, under the fatherhood of the one Supreme God Jehovah (a word which has etymological resemblance to the word *Shiva*). A religio-socio-political system develops around him which gives birth to what later divides into Islam (literally, 'surrender to God') and Judaism, which is codified by Moses.

In India, where there is growing dissatisfaction with the now rampant idolatry and confusing pantheon of 'gods', Buddha arrives (approximately 250 BC) with a humanistic approach. With basic honesty he acclaims that suffering is due to desires and that liberation involves their suppression by following the 'Noble Eightfold Path':

1. Right action
2. Right belief
3. Right aspiration
4. Right speech
5. Right livelihood
6. Right endeavour
7. Right thought
8. Right meditation

The key word of course is 'right'. But what is 'right' has been tossed back and forth between the religions and within Buddhism itself as it splintered into various sects. Without the knowledge of, or relationship with God, all attempts by souls in all cultures to do what is 'right' can resist the increasing speed of entropic downfall, but unless there is replenishment from an external source, the energy of things has to get lower and lower and the order of them more chaotic.

Next comes Christ to found the Christian 'dynasty'. He shows through his life that we should love one another as brothers and sisters and uphold the commandments of 'our Father who art in Heaven'. He also bears the message that the lost paradise will come again and that the ones who will be able to be born there are those who have 'reconciled themselves to God'. 'You have to be twice-born to enter the Kingdom of Heaven.' This is his gospel or 'good news'. The paradise that had finished only 500 years before would come again.

Shankaracharya, coming 500 years after Christ, teaches the path of renunciation, isolation and penance in founding the religion of the *Sanyasis* ('renunciates'). The leading members of this order are called *Swamis* and are revered as *gurus* or 'spiritual guides'. Physical systems of *yoga*, such as *Hatha Yoga, Kriya Yoga, Kundalini Yoga, Mantra Yoga* and so on are developed under the tutelage of the *Sanyasis* in attempts to establish the real *yoga* or link with God. The idea of God's being omnipresent is given weight by this branch. One hundred years later (about 600 AD) Mohammed starts a revival movement within Islam, which had degenerated since Abraham's time. He codifies Islam's practices in the chapters of the Koran and attempts to unify the scattered Islamic states under the banner of Allah, the one God.

The population continues to grow in geometric progression as each soul arrives and occupies its place within one or another of the religions. From one birth to another, because of different karmic accounts with other souls, some take birth in other religions where they feel completely out of place. Others are converted from one to another. The once *deity* souls themselves are dispersed all over the planet through rebirth, but the majority still remain in India. All souls seek to establish a relationship with God or some being higher than themselves but the very search takes them further into the abyss of death, confusion, waste and ultimately madness.

Iron Age, *Kaliyuga* – the age of death

The search for something higher is becoming desperate, as impurity and decadence become extreme. Human beings by this time are totally chained to the vices, creating unlimited sorrow and unrest. It is the age of utmost decline in moral, ethical and spiritual values. Conditions of chaos and anarchy under the guise of democracy have totally overtaken the system of divine monarchy. The masses are continually being incited on the basis of differences of language, religion or political belief. People are against themselves, others and nature. The world is divided and power games are rife. The actions of a caring group may benefit some but it is always at a cost to others. Religion as a basis for living is supplanted by scientific thinking. Science is a 'god' which reduces everything to material values. Perverse thinking permeates all levels of society. The poor are against the rich, blacks against whites, brothers against sisters, through oblivion of our common origin. There is total disruption in family life, which is reflected in the community, in the city, in the nation and in the world.

Towards the end of the iron age all conditions become extreme. Society becomes degraded and dehumanised. The pursuit of material ambition is held as the sole aim and object of existence. 'Eat, drink and be merry' is the catchphrase of the masses, without thought for consequences.

Respect is replaced by conceit, mistrust and sexual promiscuity. There are many demonstrations and revolutions. Power changes hands rapidly and in the final hours of the iron age, the weapons and equipment are manufactured which can bring about the physical transformation of the world. Souls are liberated from their bodies and return to the soul world. The river of history has run its full course.

The illusion of progress

When we look at the wonders of the modern technological world, the huge pulsating urban centres, the great leaps forward in medical and agricultural science and so many achievements that mark the present age, it is hard not to believe that humanity has always been progressing in every sense and that it is light-years ahead of its ancestors. How can one reconcile obvious feats with the statement that humanity has not actually been progressing but that it is now at its lowest ebb? Is there an explanation that can reconcile a truly elevated past with an apparently elevated present?

Recorded history dates back only 2,500 years and certainly within that period we have seen human beings with practically nothing, no useful tools or medicines, socially inept and with rudimentary technology, develop to their present stature, armed with the most sophisticated weaponry, means of transport and social organisation. People regard their ancestors with disdain, but they used technology which was natural and non-polluting, efficient and serviceable, rather than becoming the master. There was perfect health and no question of medicine and, as the population was small and the earth fresh, the earth naturally gave its best in fruits and vegetables; there was no question of having to till the earth with the blood and sweat that are often associated with agriculture.

From then until now agricultural methods have improved in order to satisfy a greater necessity. For the first time, the body started to experience the effects of 'wrong' action in the form of ill-health.

Medicine developed from that time, with each leap forward accompanied by wider and wider strains of disease, from the bubonic plague to AIDS. As nature ceased to respond to our needs, we had to sit down and figure out ways to extract energy from the earth to make the hard times easier. From that time on, from wheels to spaceships, from rocks to atom bombs, we have been 'progressing', but none of these efforts have brought back the lost paradise.

While we pat ourselves on the back for the electronic revolution, laserbeam weapons and so on, we are deluded into imagining that we can control our future in the same way we can control a machine or a gun. Though we may have ventured millions of miles into space, we have not advanced one millimetre in our understanding of the self. That is why modern-day progress is an illusion and why only true, lasting progress can come from God.

Confluence age, Sangamyuga – the age of illumination

When there is the absolute decline of practised truth, it is then necessary to re-establish the world of truth. The one eternal seed, *Shiva*, the one who is able to perceive all events of all time periods, comes to reveal the story of our history. It is a story of long ago but of only yesterday. That story of a world of truth, of love, joy and purity, stirs deep feelings from the long-buried past in our hearts: how these original divine human beings danced their way gradually into the stage of distress and then searched to rediscover that world. What were living memories had faded into forgotten dreams. Now, however, the vision of a united and spiritually regenerated humanity, something that all religions have dreamed about, is given concrete existence in His teaching and *yoga* with us.

Numbers

For those who like to substantiate facts with numbers: the cycle is 5,000 years, which is divided into four equal periods of 1,250 years each, for the golden, silver, copper and iron ages. In the golden age there is a maximum of eight births; in the silver age, 12 births; in the copper age, 21 births and in the iron age, 42 births, with one spiritual birth in the age of confluence. This makes a maximum total of births for a human soul to be 84 and naturally the minimum is one. The number of births that a soul has is determined by its own intrinsic purity and power.

The population at the beginning of the Golden Age is 900,000 and at the end of the iron age is 5,500,000,000.

Meditation exercises

Spinning the cycle of self-realisation
The soul world (The stage of inaction)
I am resting in my home,... a world of golden-red light... I am now aware, but am immersed in peace and silence... I am in a state of inaction, dormant... I am waiting 'back stage' before going to play my part in the world drama... The moment I descend into a body, I begin to perform action... I begin to create accounts with other souls.

The golden and silver ages (The stage of neutral action)
I am a pure soul in a new world... I am full of my original qualities... I feel no lack and so I have no desire... The sanskaras of perfection go immediately into action... No worry, hesitation or indecision... There is no difference between thought and action... My pure thoughts are spontaneous... The balance in me is reflected in the whole world... When my thoughts and actions are simultaneous, I am a natural ruler... My actions are not bondages and there is no question of doing good or bad... To whom will I do good, when all others are perfect..? I do not have the capacity for evil... This state of the soul is one of complete bliss.

The copper and iron ages (The stage of negative action)
I become body-conscious... I forget my original attributes... I am confused... My judgement about which actions will bring peace and happiness is impaired... Between thought and action the block of conscience appears... I begin to act in such a way as to cause loss and pain to myself and to others... This pain creates the desire to be free from it... Desire becomes the springboard for all my actions... With other actors on the world stage, this desire becomes the basis for all my relationships... When I act with another under the impulse of a body-conscious desire, this manifests as anger, greed, ego, lust or attachment... The immediate or long-term suffering will be experienced by the other and, by the law of reaction, that suffering will return to me in exact proportion... An account is thus created between two souls... We are bound to be in contact again to balance the account... I go further down into the spiral of suffering and desires,... more body-consciousness... In ignorance, I continue to create bondages that reinforce my ignorance... I become more and more attached to the fruits of the seeds which I sow, and I find many disappointments and deceptions... With no knowledge of my true self, I can never break this 'vicious circle'... The more I am brought into bondage, the more I seek the one who is above bondage, God... I look for release by going to others and find that they are also in bondage... They also are looking for a way out.

The confluence age (The stage of positive action)
Through the highest form of karma *I am able to balance my accounts of negative actions or 'sins' and become light... If I act as a 'world benefactor', like my Father, then the reaction is automatically beneficial... When I meditate, or have communion with God, extreme peace and bliss flow into me and through me into the world... The* yoga *I have affects the entire world... It is like the fragrance of incense... It pervades the whole room... I am able to spread the fragrance of God's love to every part of the world.*

I now fix myself in my eternal consciousness... I sit with my Baba*; I sit with God as a soul... I sit as the soul in the awareness of my eternal relationship with God... I understand that in this awareness, I can spread the fragrance of complete purity, complete love and complete peace to all souls... I understand how I can be beyond the limits of physical consciousness... I dance internally with the joy of this pure experience... I experience within me the joy, the peace, the power and the purity which will later emerge creatively in a world where every member of society expresses pure emotion.*

Now I come back to the awareness of this confluence age; the age when the soul with knowledge must act with total detachment... I move with the awareness that I am a pure soul, constantly showering gifts of peace, purity and love on all souls through good vibrations and good wishes... I maintain pure soul-conscious relations with others. I see how once before I did such action... I see how I have previously risen and fallen... So my destiny is already assured... I am merely re-creating my role for eternity... My eternal fortune flashes before me... I carry with me my constant link with God, the Supreme, the ocean of knowledge... and the seed, constantly showering happiness on my fellow souls.

Raja Yoga – regaining self-sovereignty

Time has eroded the original system of benign rulers and peaceful subjects. In the same way time has eaten into the ruling power within our own selves. Consider the intellect as the 'king', the *sanskaras* as the 'subjects' and the mind as the 'kingdom'. In the world of heaven we ruled ourselves. There was natural control of thoughts because the soul was full of love, peace, purity and power.

As these wore down with time, the impure tendencies and habits undertook a *coup d'etat*. The intellect was deposed and the *sanskaras* began to rule. Order became disorder. The previous self-sovereignty became bankrupt and uncontrolled. The intellect became weaker and virtually gave up hope of becoming ruler of the self again. While the 'subjects' ran rampant over the 'kingdom', the 'king' went into the exile of its own weaknesses.

Raja Yoga means the connection (*yoga*) by which one becomes a king (*raja*). With the power of the Almighty Authority flowing directly into the intellect, the soul, with courage, overthrows the negative *sanskaras* and again takes its rightful throne, with order and control following naturally.

*From the station of the heart to the throne of love,
Our life's journeys rise to meet the goal
That is set forever.
Like a precious jewel in a ring of eight white stones
He beckons forth.
The highest call which melts the past
Of these eternal moments moving forward.
We cease to see what effort has endured,
And do not count the time we have been away.
Found, then lost, then found again,
The cycle spins.
And He, the Liberator, can see through us
And knows our game,
Can bring our hidden virtues
To dance across our minds and into life.*

*At last you're here, dear One!
What castles we had built of sand,
Cast amid a foreign land we bore, but did not love.
Each grain a thought shaped by desire,
Made firm in action.
Imprisoned in those castled walls
We hungered for you, sweet Baba,
Grew weary in our chains
And against your gentle lapping love,
These walls do not remain.
This end befits the works,
Begins and decorates this birth
With glorious coronation.
While between these parting scenes
We choose our roles to play,
Enjoy this perfect game,
To circle round and back again.*

The stages of purity

Traditionally in India all things have been classified according to their levels of purity as either *sato*, pure or elevated; *rajo*, semi-pure, or *tamo*, impure or degraded. All souls pass through these stages, whether the soul takes a full number of births in the cycle (84) or only one birth. In the *sato* golden age all souls are *sato*, but in the *tamo*, iron age souls may be *sato, rajo* or *tamo* depending on their state of existence.

The law of cyclic repetition

To see time as cyclic and absorb the implications of this requires some deep contemplation. It is really like discovering a new dimension. If we move around the earth we eventually get back to the spot where we started. Arriving back again, we can traverse the same circumference again and again. One can imagine the difficulty that there was at the time that this was discovered, or rather rediscovered, in the 15th and 16th centuries. By limitations of perspective, it is not possible to 'see' this 'two-dimensional' movement on the surface in its three dimensions.

The soul, a non-dimensional point of conscient energy, moves and acts in the dimensions of space and in cyclic time which, with our limited consciousness, we can only see as linear. We do not have sufficient perspective to see that the line we individually trace through time in birth and rebirth brings us back to the same point we started from.

The role of God in the world drama

For pure communication with the Supreme Soul, pure knowledge is necessary. As with human relationships, the more we know about the other's role, the more affinity we can experience with them. So too, precise knowledge of God's actual role in this world endears Him to us and creates a real foundation for the complete experience of Him. As we have understood:
- God does not motivate human acts.
- God does not guide the behaviour of the elements.
- God is not a creator of matter or souls.

So, what is His creation? He performs three acts: creation, sustenance and destruction. However, this does not refer to the birth, life and death of people or things.

What are the acts of God?

In India, God is called *Karan Karavanhar*. That means He is the one who does and gets things done by others. However, this is traditionally mistaken to mean that everything moves according to His will. As our orientation is physical, we view creation as a physical phenomenon. Just a little application of common sense will tell us that God did not make human bodies out of dust. The procreators of human bodies have always been other human beings. All physical beings exist as a result of the union of the sexes in some form. If God were the giver of birth in this sense, why then should some wish to escape from life?

Likewise, if God had created this material universe, then He would also control and interfere in it constantly, creating rainstorms, droughts, plagues, good harvests, sunrises, sunsets and so on. These are all natural processes. The planets keep position because of attraction and repulsion and not because of some supernatural force. In imagining God to be generator, operator and destroyer, in the physical sense, we have utterly confused His real role.

Creation

Creation is actually the regeneration, rejuvenation or reshaping of what already exists. When the whole of humanity becomes weak spiritually, God rejuvenates the souls by imparting knowledge and divinising their intellects. He puts life energy back into souls. In that way He sows the seeds of the new golden age. He brings souls nearer to Himself and thus they come nearer to each other. In this way, He is the creator of a world of unity, peace, love and harmony on the earth.

The task of making a plan for the whole of humanity is beyond the capacity of human beings. It is the function of God, by virtue of His unlimited attributes. When peacelessness, lawlessness, disease, violence and misery threaten the entire world, the bestowal of health and abundance, purity and peace on suffering humanity becomes the task of the Supreme Soul. No one else is competent to do it. Creation is really the purification of souls, the act of establishing once again the divine order.

Nothing created is permanent. Just as when a seed is sown in a field, first the old crop must be harvested, when the new world order is being established, the old world order must be destroyed. When Shiva Baba acts as creator, there is world-scale transformation. Souls are not destroyed. Matter or nature is not destroyed. Only disease and pollution and the negative forces within humans are destroyed.

As the revealer of the laws of action, Shiva Baba must come onto the field of action and demonstrate them. He could not just remain in the soul world and perform the act of creation from there. Sending vibrations is just not enough, primarily because human beings have become so body-conscious that they are not subtle enough to pick up such vibrations. Their link with Him has been severed, and human beings through their own efforts and fantasies have not been able to reconnect themselves with Him. Besides that, He is not some sort of cosmic magician who can transform the world by an act of magic or 'will'.

He comes incognito like a 'thief in the night' as it says in the Bible, at the end of the iron age. He 'borrows' the body of the most experienced of all human souls, the first soul to enter the cycle. In India he is called *Admi* (man) or *Adi Dev*, which means the first deity. *Adi* (the first or original) is the probable root of the word 'Adam'. So, the soul of Adam, after passing through the cycle of births, again becomes the instrument for the recreation of the world of heaven. Shiva Baba is able to make full use of his experience in revealing all the secrets of the human world drama. The very fact that He comes unleashes the forces of transformation. In the act of creation of the new 'house', the destruction of the old one becomes necessary and inevitable.

Destruction

The Old Testament is full of stories of God as the destroyer, a vengeful God, destroying whole armies who dared to stand in the way of His 'chosen' ones. In the Hindu pantheon, God as the destroyer figures prominently. In different guises, sometimes as Kali, sometimes as Shankar, sometimes as Krishna, God is shown slaughtering millions. In all mythologies the aspect of God as a destroyer figures prominently.

God is not the destroyer of human beings, just as He is not the creator of human beings. He is the destroyer of evil and the creator of virtue. All these tales of huge armies being destroyed in one swipe of the Supreme's arm are allegories. For example, there is the tale of the crossing of the Red Sea by the Israelites and the subsequent destruction of their Egyptian slave masters. This tale appears in many cultures, only with different names, places and dates.

On one side, there is the land of affliction and suffering (in this case, Egypt) and, on the other side, the land of 'milk and honey', the 'promised land'. In between, there is a seemingly impassable sea, which, by the grace of God, opens up and the 'chosen ones' cross. Behind them, their former captors are drowned, as God closes the water on them. The story is obviously symbolic. The 'chosen ones', the true lovers of the true God, have the path made easier for them through His unswerving guidance. Such a one is thus able to leave the experience of suffering behind and make the journey across to the other side to a world of perfection and purity, the golden age. The weaknesses, our former 'captors', try to follow but are exterminated completely by God's help.

Others believe that God finally destroys the world because of His wrath. But it is not God that makes the nuclear bombs or natural calamities.

The Supreme Soul, in fact, merely inspires us to reach a powerful stage of meditation. It is from the centre of this fire of love and *yoga* that the vibrations of world transformation spread. This purifying influence on the consciousness of humanity actually fans the fires of the destruction of the old world. Destruction is thus a reflection of the power of *yoga*, the necessary companion of creation. This destructive aspect is symbolised by Shankar. He is shown sitting in the deep stillness of meditation; naked, to show the complete freedom from body-consciousness and conquest of evil in the self. It is said that the flames of destruction emerged from Shankar's third eye.

Sustenance

The result of knowledge and the deep fire of *yoga* is the all-virtuous state. Vishnu is a symbol of this purity and sovereignty. Vishnu is shown with four arms and represents the perfect male/female couple: pure and equal. It is the perfect couple, Lakshmi and Narayan, who rule throughout the golden age.

Vishnu also symbolises the perfect family life which acts as a sustaining force in the early part of human history. As the family life becomes more impure, so too the sustaining force in this world becomes weaker, until eventually the system breaks down completely. The four ornaments that Vishnu is holding represent four subjects that souls must absorb in order to take part in the kingdom of Vishnu. The discus denotes the knowledge of the cycle which enables pure thoughts. The conch shell represents service through spreading both the sound and vibration of spirituality. The lotus flower is a symbol of pure actions. The mace represents the completeness of victory through *yoga* over the five vices of anger, greed, ego, lust and attachment, and the conquest of the sense organs.

Thus, what Vishnu represents becomes the aim and object of human beings, ie purity in thoughts, words and actions and complete success in relating to the world around us. Many think that God is a sustainer out of his supreme generosity and that He gives us goods, wealth, health, food, water air and so on. If that were so, why would He be so unfair? Why do poverty, starvation and disease exist, if God is a sustainer and provider of all in the physical sense.

In fact, each human being earns his own livelihood. It is not God who pays the wages. Whatever fruits we earn are the results of our own efforts. God is not a physical sustainer, just as He is not a physical creator or destroyer. He sustains first of all by providing human beings with a glimpse of their own highest potential. When we have inculcated that purity through a loving relationship with Him, it is that purity which sustains the systems of the new world. God is the provider of love, peace, happiness and all the virtues. It is the absence of these which results in our systems gradually falling apart.

> *Streaming beams of light through shattered panes,*
> *Fill the room of life, with truth's warm glow.*
> *Dancing sunbeams, filled with sweet dreams,*
> *Lay to rest a sea of doubts,*
> *Let your sorrow out.*
> *Sitting 'neath the tree of life again,*
> *Fortune easy won, love's deep flow.*
> *Welcome inner sight, ambassadors of light,*
> *Challenge thrown before the weary,*
> *Well, He says, 'Come near Me. Children, come near Me.'*
> *Wearing lustrous coats, the grains of time,*
> *Dressed to call us back to innocence.*
> *Happiness His words, nectar overheard.*
> *Shaking off the chains of sadness,*
> *Let's have gladness.*
> *Pulled by knowledge, sweetly pushed by love,*
> *Soaring to the source of mercy.*
> *Sighted soldiers, filled with boldness,*
> *Hoisting flags to fly forever… to fly forever.*

The benefits of the knowledge of the cycle

In meditation the soul is able to fly above all limitations and sees and feels the reality of the golden age. If the soul allows itself to slip back into ordinary everyday consciousness, just by seeing and relating to the impure world around it, it may feel that the golden age is a fantasy. However, if there is true soul-consciousness and the experience of the original state of the soul, then the aim and object is attained. In a cycle we are merely becoming what we were. In a cycle the past is the future, and the present is the future.

Thus I am inspired to create the best types of actions now.

Meditation exercise

Spinning the cycle

I am a soul,... the seed of all my births... Now I am with my Supreme Mother and Father in our home of light... In my incorporeal form,... a point of light,... detached,... observer,... I see the vast world drama stage below... and my roles throughout the ages,... first as a deity,... pure,... light,... natural... Then I understand just how I fell and became a worshipper,... looking for You, sweet Baba,... searching through so many births,... searching,... and now I am back here with You,... from worship worthy to worshipper... and now... You are making me worthy again,... filling me with self-respect and spirituality... Oh Baba... how You have kindled my fortune!

Chapter 6 The Human World Tree

What is true religion?

'Religion' in the Western world has many unpopular connotations. There are so many instances of the use of 'religion' to excuse or disguise greed or violence, or the word has become synonymous with blind faith, meaningless rituals and fanaticism. Many establishments which propagate 'religious' principles have vested interests in money or power. As there is no shortage of souls seeking peace through religious experience, they become easy prey. By conjuring up terrifying consequences for failing to adhere to certain dogma, many religions have cut deeper divisions in our universal family.

Certainly there has been a decline in the true spirit of religion while there has been an increase in faith in the power of science. There is a feeling that, with time, everything will be explained and organised by science; that there is no need for religion. Yet, while many have turned against the traditional, institutionalised religions, the capacity and need for true religious experience remains. This section attempts to explain how the religions have reached their present stage. True religion should be the catalyst for universal unity, but we see a world falling further into divisions and the religions themselves breaking up into more and more sects and groups. History is stained by the incredible paradox of two armies fighting against each other, both of them believing that God is on their side and that He will help them conquer the other.

The sanskrit word *dharma* is inadequately translated into English as the word 'religion' (from the Latin 'religare' – to reconnect). *Dharma* refers to:

- the soul's essential nature, or *swadharma*, of peace and purity
- a life lived according to truth, duty and beauty which comes from a deeply understood relationship with God.

The existence of the soul and God are unprovable. So it comes down to a question of individual experience. On the basis of the knowledge of who and what God is and is not, what He does and does not do, we can come to an experience of this ourselves. All that is required is a clear, open mind and a deep desire to experience.

A true religion should guide one to peace in a practical way. A true relationship with God is dependent upon accurate knowledge. We are told that God is 'inaccessible and hidden from our eyes', 'a mystery'. So we are asked simply to believe in His existence. Religions based on faith alone ultimately lose the power to communicate any spiritual experience and end up as the purveyors of empty ritual.

Through our 'reconnection', God communicates the realisation of Himself and restores our true inner religion. This is something that no human being could do. He clears the path and gives us the understanding of how and why humanity has reached its present stage and what we have to do.

Religious experience

The religions propagated by human beings have tried in the main to interpret spiritual experience through experiences of their founders, saints and prophets. Sets of beliefs and rituals were constructed in the hope that the same experiences would come to them. Few have dwelt on the possibility of approaching God directly and having a first-hand experience. Not possessing the subtlety necessary for such an encounter, the majority have remained content with the inspirations received from the principal personalities of their religions. Gautama Buddha once said that we should not be concerned with the arrows but with the target to which the arrows point; that is, we should concern ourselves with the Supreme Being and not with the lives of those who point to Him.

In reality the opposite has happened and the lives of the religious founders almost completely overshadow their message. Their lives and examples have been enshrined and worshipped in such a way that the One from whom they received their inspiration and mission has been rather put aside. Christ, Mohammed, Zoroaster, Guru Nanak were all pointing to the same God, the one Father. If their followers had also looked to that One, the religions might have co-existed harmoniously.

Buddha left the whole question of a Supreme God aside because, by that stage of history, in India, there were already so many differing ideas on the nature of God. He instead concentrated on the divinity within the human soul and on the liberation from the illusions of material existence.

The Hebrews, with their long line of prophets, had unshakeable faith in the fatherhood of God, but never advanced any definitive ideas about the human soul. For them life was limited to one birth. Without the knowledge of the soul and an accurate introduction to God, everything had to rest entirely on faith in the religion of their forefathers. One of the effects of this was that each religion claimed exclusivity to the truth. Each religion considered all others to be invalid. The real God, who, in fact, is the only unifying principle, became a mere word or concept which differed from place to place and culture to culture, only serving to divide, especially where one idea of 'God' was forced upon another.

God was relegated to the background, while people discussed, debated and battled about concepts and ideas as to who or what God could be. Just as the sun has little to do with darkness on the earth, God has nothing to do with the darkness of our ignorance. The sun continues to shine regardless of which part of the earth is passing through the night. It stays in the 'background' while we try to adjust ourselves to the darkness. No matter what forms of lighting are devised for the darkness, not one can compare with the sun itself.

Spiritual lights which came in the form of different founders, prophets and saints, like so many candles, some brighter than others, have, in the long run, been poor substitutes for the sun of knowledge Himself. Just as the language of mathematics is the same for the whole world, the language of souls is one. There is one reality which binds us together and lies beyond the bickerings and divisions. The basis of true religious experience and the aim and goal of all religions, however differently expressed, has been to realise God and His qualities. Surely then, the most elevated of all spiritual practices is to have communion with Him as He is and to have unshakeable access to His qualities.

The idea that God comes to humanity as a protector has been a common principal theme of all religions. But just how and when He comes, and for what purpose, has created controversy. There have been so many so called 'incarnations of God' that one is left wondering why the world has become so degraded despite this 'divine intervention'. Without doubt, the spiritual and moral principles shown to us by Christ, Buddha, Abraham and other spiritual masters have appealed to something higher in us. Our mere emotional involvement, however, has neither helped us to stop the world's decline nor to overcome our weaknesses and live as God's children on this earth – which is the common knowledge they have all tried to preach.

Negative emotions are more connected to the physical senses than with any spiritual sense. So, when principles are forgotten and all that is left are emotions, there follow degradation and fanaticism. One can easily see how the division of society into different sectarian and religious groups has caused misunderstanding and conflict when based on body-consciousness. The dividing lines between peoples and nations are their rituals, mythologies, customs and beliefs.

The tree of religions – a synopsis of the world drama

The cycle of history can also be expressed in the form of a tree. The 'Tree of Life' is an analogy used in all religions. It symbolises the beginning, growth and decay of civilisation. God the Supreme, *Shiva*, is the seed, the essence from which the whole tree grows. From the seed come the roots, the foundation from which the tree grows. The seed contains within it the complete knowledge of the tree. Those souls who take this knowledge and assimilate it in their practical lives form the roots. From their pure actions a healthy young shoot emerges which later becomes the trunk.

The trunk – the golden and silver ages

The trunk is formed by the souls of the golden and silver ages. Its oneness is reflected in one religion, one culture, one language and one system of government. Since each soul is perfectly fulfilled there is no search for any higher values and even God is not remembered. It is the first half of the cycle; the enjoyment of the fruits of one's efforts towards self-realisation and perfection during the previous confluence age.

Each one is an embodiment of God's qualities to a certain degree and hence has no need to call out to God. There are no churches, temples, priests, scriptures, rituals or any of the paraphernalia of the path of worship. Religion is their practical life, the temples their bodies and these residents of heaven themselves imbued with God's qualities, are later called 'gods' and 'goddesses' and 'deities'.

These are the very 'gods' of our legends. In all the ancient civilisations they were venerated and this is why, even though the names change from place to place, the various mythologies speak about the same happenings.

The branches – the copper age

This is the age of worship and duality. The period of *adharma* or irreligiousness begins. True values are gradually replaced by artificial ones. Harmony gives place to conflict and competition. In an effort to regain the bliss of the former state of the world, we begin to search. Out of the search, religions spring up. The solid trunk begins to branch out. Having lost the power that purity gave us, we turn to the One whose impression is deepest in us from 2,500 years before, at the end of the previous cycle.

It was Shiva, the Seed, who had bestowed on humanity the kingdom of paradise, the golden and silver ages. When confusion breaks out at the beginning of the copper age, we turn our minds automatically to Him in the form of pure, single-minded worship. Gradually the population increases and the extent of the search spreads. It is during this time that other parts of the world are explored and colonised, as groups of human beings travel here and there in an effort to regain the art of living in peace and harmony.

The prophet souls, Abraham, Buddha, Christ, Mohammed and so on, establish their various religions. Though each professes universal kinship and dedication to one God, there is no universal application of their teachings. Each holds a different aim and set of beliefs. The trunk religion thus branches across the world into many new ruling dynasties. New languages develop. The harmony the world once knew is shattered. We enter into an era of strife which later becomes fully-fledged war. After the prophets die, their religions are supported by scriptures and a faith based on the glorification of their lives and words.

The twigs and leaves – the iron age

This is the age of ignorance and darkness. Blind faith leads souls further into degradation and hence further away from God, the seed of truth. Almost anything is worshipped in an attempt to bring back the former purity and power. More branches appear on the tree. The four main religions of Hinduism, Islam, Buddhism and Christianity sub-divide into more branches. They too become diversified and disunified.

In this spiritual confusion many cults, sects and 'isms' also emerge. Both religion and philosophy become more materialistic. The last twigs of the tree are extremely distant from the seed. Our lives and relationships with others become devoid of real love, peace and happiness. Life is controlled by vice. The status of women is demeaned and they are treated as objects of sexual indulgence.

Societies develop, motivated by the ever-growing demand for material goods. People become slaves to their desires. Differences of opinion dominate individual families, communities and nations. Religion becomes involved in the accumulation of wealth and temporal power. Science develops the means of mass destruction. The world is divided by colour, sects, religion and politics. We are tied in the bondages of culture, family, tradition and legislation.

Natural calamities increase. Disease, premature death, accidents, poverty and mental suffering make life a veritable 'hell'. People become enslaved by their sense organs and yet pray to God to remove the suffering. However, while the ever-increasing peacelessness turns more and more people towards God, without knowing Him, they remain powerless. This need provides fertile ground for the emergence of 'pseudo-gods' or 'god-men' who add to the confusion with new and more fashionable interpretations of traditional teachings. People are made to perform astounding rituals, either inspired by some boon offered or some fear. Each soul hangs as helplessly as a leaf on the twig of what it believes in.

The period of search – the path of 'bhakti' during the copper and iron ages

Science involves a search for truth and meaning in the outer world. Religion involves a search for truth and meaning in one's inner personal world. In the scientific search for understanding, we have literally looked under every stone, striving to classify and categorise all material things, hoping that, in so ordering it, we could bring order to ourselves. However, even though we finally come to split an atom, truth still escapes us. Since we began to identify the self with the body and God with the material world, believing God to be the creator of matter and to be omnipresent, we have placed too much emphasis on physical practices. None of those methods have eradicated the accumulation of negative *sanskaras* in the soul.

At the beginning of the copper age when internal conflict began to develop, naturally we searched for what seemed to be free of conflict. The prophets and saints, these 'extra-ordinary' humans, became the objects of worship. Various philosophies and models for life were preached and written down but there was not enough strength in the ordinary souls to put them into practice. The libraries filled up with books and yet the miseries and conflicts increased. Knowledge is the fruit of the search. In other words, those who search do not know, and those who know, cease to search.

Finally the ocean of knowledge, the Supreme Soul Shiva, reveals that true science and true religion are related and need to be united to create a new world. He gives us a simple understanding of the eternal laws. When the seed of the tree comes, the search is over. The souls that originally belonged to the trunk of the golden and silver ages leave the branches and return to the seed, becoming the roots underground from which the new tree grows and the eternal play revolves once again.

The scriptures

For 2,500 years the purity of the deities only slightly declines. When they lose it, the natural understanding of what God taught them at the end of the previous cycle begins to emerge through intuition and inspiration within certain souls. These *sanskaras* manifest in a world completely different from the world in which God originally inspired them. Moreover, these are subjective and individual and hence are without the power to transform. Without the complete objectivity that God alone has, no scripture or sacred work could communicate the same powerful message, either because the inspirations were out of context or were intermingled with subjective input.

At the time of writing the scriptures, God was not speaking to us directly but it was our own subjective feelings about Him that were speaking to us. For instance, how could God have said 'I am omnipresent'? If He were, how could there be a voice? God's presence has always been an area of great misunderstanding, and this phrase 'God is omnipresent' could only have been a human attempt to explain God's greatness, or to feel greater proximity to Him.

The saints, sages and scribes who penned their inspirations and formulated the world's scriptures had the problem of trying to relate what they wrote to the world. As time and conditions were changing from the copper age to the iron age, they had continually to make adjustments and readjustments in order to suit social and theological changes. And now, we shy away from the incredible amount of scriptural material and think, if it were truly God who was the source of our sacred texts, He couldn't have succeeded better in confusing us. While the messages are inspiring, especially concerning the virtues, the actual process of acquiring them is seldom touched upon. The words 'God' and 'soul' permeate these great works, while no exact descriptions of the 'soul' and 'God' are given. The result is that we become acutely aware that we should be better, but without the power to put all these 'Thou shalts' into practice.

Paths of spiritual pursuit

There are basically three paths of search:

1. The Path of Renunciation (Sanyas)
In every religion there have been those who have renounced the worldly life and have dedicated their lives to the pursuit of God through penance and prayer. This necessitated an end of family life for the monks, nuns, *gurus* and *sanyasis*, who took such vows.

2. The Path of Worship (Bhakti)
Most people are worshippers of one sort or another. The path of worship includes all the customs, rites, religious practices, chanting, modes of prayer, scriptures, texts and so on.

3. The Path of Knowledge (Gyan)
The path of knowledge is the fruit of both worship and true renunciation. This knowledge is not contained in any scripture. It includes the knowledge of God, the soul, this world and the worlds beyond, the world drama, its beginning, duration, theme and cyclic repetition. It explains the story of the rise and fall of all souls, and how the soul, whichever religion it belongs to, can have direct communion or *yoga* with the Father of all souls. It explains the complete philosophy of cause and effect as it applies to human souls and all that is necessary for the purification of souls.

The students learning from the Supreme Teacher are not concerned with renouncing worldly responsibilities or family life. They renounce only anger, greed, ego, lust and attachment. When they come to know God through understanding, the search is over. Instead of continuing to worship purity in someone else, they set about becoming pure themselves.

Are there many paths to God, or one?

It is said that just as there are many paths to the top of a mountain, you can travel any spiritual path to attain God. Realising God, however, is not the same as climbing a mountain. This idea presupposes that the soul would, by its own efforts, attain God. This is like asking a patient on his death bed to regain normal health and then go to see the doctor. If the soul could purify itself, then God's undeniable role of purifier or saviour would have no meaning. Actually, everyone is searching for a path to God.

The path is knowledge. The branches of the search are not many paths to the top of the same mountain. Rather, looking at the tree, we can see how they have been leading away from God.

God thus has to uplift all souls of all faiths and religions. He comes when the tree has reached full maturity, when the conflicting ideas about who God is and what truth is are extreme. God, the Supreme Soul, is one and the path to Him can only be revealed by Him. He alone has the imperishable knowledge that transcends time and space. Only He can guide human souls to complete victory over all suffering, physical and mental.

Spiritual knowledge

The difference between the religions and different cultures is nothing more than a difference in social customs, rituals and myths. Spiritual knowledge, on the other hand, is the same for the whole of humanity. The basic principle of human consciousness and existence is one and the same for all. There is no variation on truth.

See the tree again as an example. If it could think, it would probably object to losing its leaves every autumn. But the laws of nature hold true, whether the tree likes it or not, agrees to it or not, understands it or not. There are certain immutable laws which govern the changing of the 'seasons' of human history and, whether we understand them or not, agree to them or not, they hold true.

The leaves of the tree of humanity are many, but the tree is one. The seed is one. The truth about the tree is one. The law that determined its birth, growth, decay, death and rebirth is one. God is the revealer of that truth. It is He who re-establishes the golden age; who changes human beings into viceless deities; who plants the sapling of the real and highest religion, that of divinity. When there is untold human suffering and uncountable schisms it is time for the Mother and Father of all to uplift humanity.

The roots of change – the confluence age

The tree reaches its optimum growth at the end of the iron age and various factors inherent in the scheme of things are brought into play. The tree is very old. The roots themselves have reached total decay. The truth has disappeared and all that remain are a tangled mass of branches –

religions, languages, cultures and ideologies. God as the Creator comes into being. He knows that in order to plant a new tree, He has to prepare the roots anew.

Just as an ordinary tree's seed and roots work unseen, the part of the Supreme Soul and souls instrumental for world transformation, are also largely unseen. While the iron age is reaching its climax, the Creator is doing His work.

The fifth age, the age of confluence, is in fact two confluences – the meeting of the souls and God, and the meeting of the old world and the new. Both the creation of the new golden-aged world and that of its necessary corollary, the destruction of the old iron-aged world, are sparked off by the advent of the Supreme Being, the only soul whose power never diminishes and who is never born into the cycle of history.

He comes to reactivate the 'root-souls', those very souls who had participated in the creation of the tree at the end of the previous cycle and, who had later taken birth during the golden and silver ages. He rejuvenates those souls by reminding them who they are, and through them, His message spreads to all souls of all religions.

Brahma and Brahmins

It is crucial at this time that God's message is clear. Inspirations or intuitions would be too open to influence, subjectivity or mistakes. For all the 'root-souls' to come together they need one coherent and powerful voice; and so, Shiva adopts a body.

He descends into the body of Brahma, an elderly experienced person whom He can use immediately for the transmission of knowledge. Brahma not only becomes the medium for knowledge but also the finest example. His life becomes a reflection of these highest teachings and thus an inspiration for us to follow. Through Brahma the Supreme Soul gives human souls a spiritual birth.

In a figurative sense it could be said that God took a handful of 'dust' and breathed life into it creating Adam and through Adam the rest of humanity came into being. The 'dust' is what the human soul had become, full of impurities, and the breath of life is the knowledge that the soul requires in order to love again and restore its full potential of purity and peace. This applies to the soul of Brahma in the first place and through him the Supreme Soul puts life back into all the self-forgotten souls.

The personal experience of this purely spiritual creation is truly wonderful. Through the 'breath' of God's knowledge the soul experiences total spiritual rebirth; a new mind, a new vision, a new dimension of living, in fact such a transformation that nothing of the old self can remain at all.

Personal experience – on being a Brahmin

When I first perceived that through this knowledge a remarkable transformation was taking place internally, there naturally came a moment of decision: am I truly one of these souls who can act as an instrument of God in the establishment of the golden-aged world? Do I have sufficient surrender and humility to recognise that it is truly God who is teaching me these things? I took a deep breath, pushed my head against the wind of possible obstacles and decided that this was really the only way in which I could create my fortune, forever. Resounding in my mind at the time was: it's now or never. God only comes once a cycle and my efforts will determine my next cycle. So I may as well make the most of it this time around.

I could see how much my decision and recognition were vital factors. To recognise that God's work is happening at this moment, and that I can directly benefit from His powers and qualities gave me the courage to take this step into the infinite.

There was a kind of death of my old personality and an immense feeling of satisfaction in being a Brahmin. A Brahmin is a soul who recognises Shiva Baba, a soul who takes spiritual birth through the mouth of Brahma and follows the highest code of conduct in order to serve humanity spiritually. Traces of the past personality still appear from time to time but I feel that, since Baba is my companion and His knowledge my weapons, victory in the battle against all negative tendencies is assured. After all, a battle valiantly fought brings the sweetest victory.

The knowledge that now is the confluence age entirely altered my perception of time. Of course, looking at the repetition of the cycle I could easily say, Whatever I became last cycle is what I'll become now, so there's no need to make effort, but, with all the materials provided by Baba, I could see the trap in such reasoning. Even to drink water I have to make some effort. So to become all-virtuous and completely viceless like the beings of the golden age, effort has to be accordingly greater.

With the third eye opening wider and wider, the present drama is perfectly understandable because Baba has shown me the developments which have led to this age of chaos. And the future pure world will be the result of assimilating His inheritance now. Now seems so important because the casting for the new world is going on. Seeing the value of this time has allowed me to savour face-to-face a meeting with my Supreme gentle Father. Even in the golden age the beings do not have such luck.

Without ourselves, without our God,
Forced to substitute
Worshipworthiness with worship,
Reality with statues.
Images of higher hopes venerated,
Degenerated.
Christ, Buddha, Mohammed and others tried
To mend our broken minds.
Stumbling, shaken, we went on pilgrimages,
Searching for the One we vaguely remembered
To be the Liberator, God Shiva.
Trying to recall His image and value,
But the golden thread had been broken.
Making buildings to catch a spirit that wasn't there.
Performing rituals as dry reminders of a former reality.
Reaching for the essence,
But remaining empty-handed.
Down and down we plunge like madmen
In the night, without the sight to see each birth,
A step further into the night.
Many steps and many births.
And still the gap between You and us was widened.
Until You came, as a cycle ago and
A cycle hence.
You came, Sweet Father,
When our life's light had almost flickered out,
Enfolded us with streams of might,
Gave us place in your unlimited heart,
To carry us to the pilgrim's peak.
Our minds had worn self-scorn
Like a heavy coat, with pockets full of lead.
You took it off, revealing naked soul,
Uncaged from its uncertainty,
And free to fly with You.
O long-lost One,
Take me.

Each soul illumined by
His breath of life;
A step towards blessedness.
Each added tragedy
In a world of death;
A step towards its grave.
The new simply overtakes the old.

Meditation exercise

The cycle and the tree

Putting the knowledge of the cycle and the tree together, I come firstly to a realisation of the time... Now and only now is the time that I can rise up out of the depths of my own ignorance and create my part for the next cycle... I see the contrast between the old world and the new, the impure world and the pure, and am inspired to cut the ropes that keep the boat of the soul tied to the shores of the iron age, knowing that every effort I make now will create loss or credit for many lives to come. Seeing my own role throughout the tree, I feel an incredible security with the knowledge of my own 'raison d'etre'... Firmly anchored in this self-faith, I see the myriad roles that I and others have played and am instilled with a sense of detachment... I was a deity in the golden age,... a divine being. Little by little I lost both my crowns; the halo of purity and the crown of temporal authority... I became a worshipper, a beggar for peace... I grew with the tree and lost sight of the trunk, by trying to comfort myself in the branches, the man-made religions... Then Baba came to explain it all to me. Seeing it from His point of view, I can see just how perfect the drama is.

I feel like a person who has fished all his life in the same spot without even imagining that the water passing by his feet had a history of its own; a pure phase, an impure phase, a pure phase again... I can see how body-consciousness prevents me from seeing the perfection of creation and how soul-consciousness, seeing myself as a soul who has passed through the history of this world, allows me to have a bird's eye view of the whole process of creation.

I can see how I myself am like a tree too... I started as a seed in the soul world. Then I came here and became a part of the trunk: the golden and silver ages... During this time I was in harmony and there was unity within myself. Then the internal divisions began with the coming of the copper age, as different desires started to pull the intellect this way and that... 'The answer is here.' 'No, it's there!' 'Peace is in this!' 'No, it's in that.' 'Come here!' 'Go there!' 'Do this.' 'Do that.' 'No.' 'Yes.' 'No.' 'Yes.'

This was the beginning of the branches of my confusion... I grew and grew *in this way, birth by birth with more and more complications, the branches threading the webs of my anxiety... Now the Seed of it all is explaining to me how it all came to pass, how I too am a seed in my original form... Knowing this, I can leave the branches and twigs of useless and impure thoughts... With the knowledge of the cycle and the tree and the recognition of the master of the tree, Shiva Baba, I can truly become a traveller of the three worlds.*

Trinetri – the third eye of wisdom and Trilokinath – master of the three worlds

We have seen how the cycle spins from new to old and to new again. We have seen how the birth, growth, decay and the rebirth of humanity take place from the tree. Using this vision in soul-consciousness can be termed as being *trinetri*, three-eyed. The inner eye, or third eye, of knowledge has opened. Also, with the knowledge of the past, present and future, the soul becomes *trikaldarshi*, knower of the three aspects of time.

When we see Baba's three-fold function of creation, sustenance and destruction, we understand the *trimurti*, the three stages, or when we come to know of the three worlds and use that knowledge to travel beyond the attractions and repulsions of the physical world, this experience is called being *trilokinath*, master of the three worlds.

To meet Shiva Baba one has to fly to His home. To plunge into that silent expanse of golden-red light and experience the completeness of the incorporeal stage is, without doubt, the most rewarding of all meditational endeavours. But such an experience is really only possible when seated in meditation with great concentration. To see the soul as a point of divine light and to feel Shiva Baba as a point also but, at the same time, as an unlimited ocean of virtues, is certainly the highest experience in meditation. This stage of meditation is attainable during those moments of complete retreat from the world of sound and activities.

Trilokinath also means to be able to use our three states of being:

1. The incorporeal state: the soul in its original stage in the soul world.

2. The subtle body: Each of us has a subtle form which can be experienced through meditation. The experience for some individuals (those who can go into trance) is very tangible but, for the majority, the immense feeling of lightness, detachment and increased perception mean that the soul is taking on the subtle or angelic form. It has the same appearance as the physical body but it is made of light.

3. The physical body: the one we know and have grown to identify

ourselves with. When we know of these other two states of being we really can see the physical body's function of not only being the instrument of the soul but the instrument to perform beneficial actions.

The subtle regions – Angelic Brahma

For meditation, during our daily routine we have to become cognisant of the subtle regions. It is not only those with the gift of going into trance who can experience those regions.

The subtle regions have three zones. It has been depicted that three divine entities, the *trimurti*, reside there. The first is called *Brahmapuri*, where the angelic Brahma stays for the work of creation. Angelic Brahma is the soul of Brahma in its perfect stage, yet still retaining the subtle light form of the physical body. The next zone is *Vishnupuri*, where the soul can have the experience of its future perfect part in the golden-aged world. The third zone is *Shankarpuri* where the soul can enter into such a powerful and detached stage of meditation that its rays reach back to the physical plane, adding fuel to the flames of destruction of all that is old and impure.

The subtle regions in fact only exist at the confluence age, specifically so that souls can train themselves to use their subtle bodies and thus move onto an unlimited plane of service. It can also be considered the meeting place of the present stage of effort-maker and our future deity form. As the name suggests, they are three zones subtly wrapped around the physical plane and performing the tasks of creation, sustenance and destruction respectively.

The subtle stage of meditation

As well as having the incorporeal meeting with Shiva Baba in the soul world, one can also meet Him through the angelic form of Brahma in the subtle regions. Shiva Baba has never experienced birth and the trials and tribulations of life on earth. So for guidance on day-to-day matters we turn to Brahma. When we put ourselves before these two souls whom we lovingly call *avyakt* (subtle or angelic) BapDada, (*Bap* refers to Shiva Baba, the Supreme Soul, and *Dada* to Brahma, the elder brother of human souls), we feel ourselves plucked out of the material swirl of sounds and events and become weightless and costumed in light.

We can sit in this subtle stage in order to ask questions or for guidance and get up again with the answer clearly in our minds. It is a stage we can easily keep with us while doing our duties. Lightness and a type of detached alertness, while being totally relaxed, are the consequences of staying in this avyakt stage, permitting us to slip into the higher incorporeal or seed stage whenever time permits.

To be able to move easily between the three regions is to be *trilokinath*. The ideal stage is to stay in the middle region while acting so that, when necessary, the soul can go into the incorporeal state and be completely recharged. At the same time the soul remains a detached observer of the events taking place around it in the physical world.

Meditation exercise

Using the subtle form

I am a soul,... totally concentrated on the throne in between the eyebrows,... radiating light,... becoming totally detached... I withdraw... I feel power surging through me, filling even the body with subtle light... Nothing physical,... no sounds here... I am in front of my Father Shiva Baba,... glowing powerfully in the forehead of the angelic form of Brahma,... the father of humanity,... the elder brother of the human race,... whose smile spells universal love... Shiva Baba's completely loving look pierces the heart of the soul... and the only appropriate word wells up in my mind... Baba, I am your child... You remind me of my speciality... You remind me of the unlimited love You have for me... I am before You, naked,... my weaknesses unrobed... You know me as I am... Oh Baba, I can hide nothing from You nor do I want to... I just want the warmth of this lap of light and love... I am in my subtle body of light... receiving your divine drishti *(vision),... burning through the soul,... purifying... filling me with the inspiration to serve humanity on this subtle level... to help You in generating the work of establishing the new world.*

The seed stage

I adopt my incorporeal form as a soul,... a tiny seed,... the seed of all my births,... of all the extensions of thoughts... All the branches of desires and emotions related to the present and other lives are called back to the seed that I am... I am in the original home... with my almighty Father before me,... the seed of the human world tree,... a radiant orb of supreme bliss and wisdom... In Your presence You bring my own pure qualities to the surface of my consciousness... I am a seed of world benefit,... radiating my original qualities,... no longer creating thoughts... but lost in pure experience.

Chapter 7 The Essence of Raja Yoga

Full meaning of *Raja Yoga*

The meaning of the word *yoga* should not be reduced merely to a physical discipline. For the uninitiated westerner, *yoga* conjures up images of complicated body-bending, saffron-robed *yogis* or *fakirs* who make their living, proving mind over matter, by calmly sitting on beds of nails or allowing themselves to be buried under the ground for hours on end.

The highest meaning of *yoga* is concentration of the mind in order to attain a mental and spiritual link with God. A true *yogi* is one who is devoted and dedicated to God alone and remains in constant awareness of Him.

Yoga is derived from the Sanskrit root *yog* which means 'link' or 'union', and *raja* means literally 'king'. So *Raja Yoga* signifies the king of unions, or the link between the soul and the Supreme Soul through which the soul becomes the controller of its own mind, intellect and *sanskaras* and consequently of its physical body. Raja Yogis, because of their access to God and through self-control, have the mental stability and heightened perception of life that enable them to remain the controller of every situation that presents itself.

Raja Yoga implies that those practising it behave in a royal manner. They are calm, composed and silence-loving, free from the disease of worry and the stress of fear. They become 'carefree kings' unaffected by the sharp contrasts of sorrow and joy, gain and loss, success and failure, praise and defamation. Their royalty and wisdom do not permit them to violate the laws of nature or the laws of God. They are utterly relaxed and yet completely alert.

The Raja Yoga that is commonly known throughout the world was collated and systematised by an Indian sage, Patanjali, about 2,000 years ago. It is also known as *Astanga Yoga*, that is, the Yoga of Eight Limbs, referring to the eight parts into which it is divided. Though he stresses that the object of *yoga* is to establish the soul in its true nature, he attaches little importance to the pivotal role of God in yogic practice. Though in Patanjali's *Yoga Sutras* (treatise on *yoga*) God is introduced as a special being, Purush Vishesha, above all kinds of sufferings and bondages of actions, the immortal and unborn, the supreme and original teacher,

Patanjali nowhere states that the object of *yoga* is to forge a mental link with this Supreme Soul. He merely uses *yoga* to concentrate and control the various modifications of the mind. For him God is just one of many possible objects of concentration.

Two of the eight limbs which develop the concentration that Patanjali says is the aim of *yoga*, are *asana* (physical postures) and *pranayama* (breath control). However, it is a misconception that in order to discipline the mind, one has first to discipline the body and control the senses. For those who practise Raja Yoga, there is the experience that, by first disciplining the vagaries of the mind and establishing the consciousness of one's true identity, there is automatic control over the sense organs.

The word *yoga* has been used to describe an entire range of human exertions and postures, intended to achieve inner peace and happiness. Although these bring harmony within the body, the ancient *yoga,* in fact, is only that practice which calms the restless mind by direct union of the soul with God. Through that union, we change, the world changes, the ages come and go and we forget how to have *yoga* with Him. He has to come and teach us again and show us how the energy of the mind can easily be redirected into constructive rather than destructive channels.

Yoga means remembrance

Wherever we focus our minds it can be said, in a loose sense, that we are having *yoga* or a mental connection. So, whenever we remember someone or something, we are having *yoga* with that person or thing. Inner peace depends on whom or what our yoga or mental connection is with and not on the posture of the body.

In our search for love, peace and happiness, the mind has focused on many temporary and limited things and relationships, all of which have only dissipated energy and broken its attention and concentration. Of all the possible mental connections, the highest and most constant is with God. It is that which is called *Raja Yoga*.

God – the teacher of Raja Yoga

Any deep study of comparative religions will yield that:
- our real nature is divine
- the aim of religion is to realise this
- all religions indicate a common origin and so have many points of agreement

First, the original state of each soul is peace, love and happiness. Second, ever since we left the golden and silver ages, we have been trying to regain that state of harmony. It is the third aspect, however, that is most interesting. Why do all religions point back to a common origin? The religions that surfaced after the fall of the silver age, 2,500 years ago, have been attempts to regain the forgotten states of peace and purity.

Almost every religion looks to God as being the revealer of the truth about humanity. This means that, at some time, there must have been some manifestation of this. As we look at the tree of life, we can see how the branches of humanity have only been growing further and further away from the seed.

God, as the seed, remains the essence of the knowledge of the tree. It is that essence that human beings seek. Five thousand years ago, God revealed that essence. The souls who took birth in the golden and silver ages were divinised. For the following 2,500 years, the world enjoyed the results of that knowledge: perfect harmony and bliss. Then, when divinity declined, the path of searching began, but instead of that real and living relationship with God, the real *yoga*, we fell back on substitutes: rituals, penances, pilgrimages, scriptures and worship. The efforts to go beyond the problems of existence created more and more complications, problems, conflicts and finally even wars.

Raja Yoga is the system by which God restores and rejuvenates souls with His own divine attributes. Through the power of souls' communion with God, the world is changed.

The soul communes with God directly

The ability to experience Raja Yoga is natural for every soul, but body-consciousness has severed that link and made us forget, just as a rusty needle cannot be attracted by a magnet. When I focus my mind and receive an immediate reciprocal response, I am able to take my mind away from the cycle of worldly thoughts and fly into the realms of ecstasy with Him.

Yoga – relationship with God

A living relationship between two people develops through each one's knowing and thinking good things about the other. When I know God and think about Him, I develop the most loving and rewarding of relationships. I know His eternal name, spiritual form and divine attributes. I know where He dwells. This is essential for any purposeful relationship with God, in exactly the same way as knowing the name, address, form, characteristics and occupation of someone are the basic requirements for any meaningful relationship. By assuming God to be everywhere, in everyone, it is impossible to enjoy any effective relationship with Him. On the other hand, as soon as I remember Him as a source of light and might, as Shiva (seed, point of light, benefactor), dwelling in the silent world of souls, a connection can be forged and I can be recharged with His qualities. As I come to understand the implications of this eternal relationship and eternal game with other souls, my love deepens and I am drawn closer.

The closer the relationship, the more easily I am reminded of it. Thus I can stay in *yoga* or communion for long periods, filled with loving and powerful thoughts, with this becoming a totally natural state of being. As the experience of achievement grows, the relationship grows. As the relationship grows, so does the achievement, and I spiral upward to become like Him: loving, peaceful and powerful. I see how this relationship is truly unique. At the same time it becomes more intimate and God Shiva becomes *Baba*, my father. Baba fulfils our basic requirements in life: for love, learning and improvement. He is my eternal Father, and also teacher and spiritual guide. He is totally selfless and only adopts us for our own improvement and, through us, for the improvement of other souls.

He is the infallible friend and companion who never lets the soul down, never sees the soul's wrongs but sees it in its perfect stage. He is the merciful and compassionate Mother whose sweetness trickles into me, the soul, and there is just the will to stay forever in the Mother's unlimited lap. He is the loving Father, whose directions are for my benefit, which I follow with obedience and respect. He is like a son, to whom I give everything I have and sacrifice myself. He is the spiritual surgeon who knows exactly the anatomy of the soul and how to extract all disease.

You are the Boatman who calms my life
From the shores of death
To the land of Your light.
You are the Gardener who tends to my needs,
Encourages the flowers, destroys all the weeds
You are the Lighthouse and we are returning
To the land long-forgotten,

> To the place we'd been yearning for
> You are the Jeweller
> You make me a diamond,
> A thing of great beauty;
> Forever to shine on.

Basis of Raja Yoga

Soul-consciousness

We can experience God only through thought, and thoughts depend on the consciousness we have. Pure thoughts which flow from soul-consciousness bring us closer to God. Impure thoughts, created by body-consciousness, lead us away from Him and therefore the *yoga* is broken.

The soul prepares itself for meditation with firm, pure thoughts: 'I am a soul, separate from my body. I am an actor playing my part through this costume, in this eternal drama of life. My original home is with Shiva Baba in the soul world.' Such thoughts establish and maintain a state of soul-consciousness or self-awareness and take us away from grossness and bondage. In fact, soul-consciousness is the basis for any spiritual attainment.

God-consciousness

When we establish a child-father relationship, we come closer to God. Instead of 'God Almighty, up there' and 'I, the sinner, down here', by thinking, 'I am a soul and He is the Supreme Soul, my father', rapport is established. The rust of all inferiority complexes is dissolved away in the fire of love.

Since Baba is the power of love and source of divine virtues for all souls, we are entitled to these qualities as His immortal children. Our thoughts dwell on His attributes as the ocean of peace, knowledge, power, purity and love and the relationship intensifies.

Practice of Raja Yoga

Raja Yoga is natural and easy. It just involves thoughts or mental 'postures'. Rather than shutting the eyes, we shut the mind to worldly, limited thoughts and concentrate on Shiva Baba. This practice of meditating with eyes open may seem strange at first but, after some time, it becomes very natural. The advantages of learning from the start to meditate in this way are many. Since it is a spiritual practice rather than a physical one, it can easily accompany all of the activities we become involved in during the day. We don't have to stop what we are doing, any more than we would, in order to remember a loved one, or one's mother or father. We only have to think of Him, as He is. When the work we are doing requires a minimum of mental attention, we can meditate, while working, without any difficulty.

For a deeper experience of *yoga* with Baba, it is sufficient to find a comfortable seat. If you can sit cross-legged on the floor, well and good, but even then, it is not necessary to close the eyes. If you are with a group of people practising Raja Yoga, there is generally someone conducting the meditation. That person sits in front while the others rest their gaze, in a natural way, at a point between the eyebrows. The person leading meditation looks at each one, in turn, in the same way. This is called *drishti* or spiritual vision. Gazing easily upon the point in the body where the soul sits and seeing the other as a soul and not a body, while at the same time remembering the Supreme Soul, gives a powerful boost to the novice and creates a feeling of real brotherly love among more experienced meditators.

If you are seated in meditation alone, keep the eyes open but unfixed on anything in particular or, if you have a picture of Shiva Baba's form you can rest your gaze on that, bearing in mind that it is only an aid and has no importance other than symbolic. Meditating with eyes open trains the soul to be ever-ready in the face of all obstacles, relaxed yet alert.

Besides, closing the eyes might lead one astray into the world of sleep. When we are conscious of God, we remain relaxed and refreshed. Tiredness and tension melt away.

> *Face to face,*
> *The meeting place*
> *In the mind's eye.*
> *Heart-to-heart,*
> *You fill my part*
> *To the highest high.*
> *Impressions for eternity, my Love.*
> *Recorded for all history, my Love.*
> *I couldn't think You'd come to me so simply*
> *And treat me to the sweetness of Your words.*
> *Mind to mind,*

You clear the line
To your treasure store.
You and I, embraced in the thought,
Forever more,
Sealed to Truth eternally, my Love.
Living once again in Light, my Love.
I couldn't think You'd come to me so simply
And treat me to the magic of Your words.

Stages of meditation

Initial stage

Trying to harness the jumpy mind and turn it in one direction is not easy but, with patience and perseverance, it can be done. Many thoughts, quite unrelated to spiritual effort, pull the soul as it attempts to concentrate.

Meditation is like a 'pilgrimage of remembrance'. It is a spiritual journey, the destination of which is the living and loving relationship with God. On a train journey, the passenger waits out the ride patiently because he knows that all he has to do is to remain seated and he will arrive. No matter how many interesting scenes pass by the window, none are sufficiently interesting for him to jump out of the window! If he did, the train would continue without him and he would miss his destination. In the same way the soul initiates the journey of meditation.

I first create my aim firmly in mind. Once the aim is clear, I create thoughts about it. Unrelated or negative thoughts, no matter how ugly or attractive, should just pass the 'window' of the mind, and be replaced by good and noble thoughts about the self, God, the world drama and the benefits of knowledge.

After some initial struggle, the wandering mind tends to rest and concentration improves steadily. Pure thoughts replace negative or useless ones. It just requires some determination. In this initial stage we can imagine the mind like a flooded plain and we are only starting 'mop-up operations'. This stage represents the first attempts to channel the 'water', in this case, the energy of thought, into one direction.

Meditation

Soon I am able to enter meditation. I am able to channel thoughts in the direction of God but it is still more of an intellectual exercise than a complete relationship. I am able to feel detached from the body and the physical world but there is effort in creating elevated thoughts. This stage manifests in daily activities in an increased soul-consciousness and detachment. This, in turn, eliminates negative thoughts and enables me to exercise a greater control over speech and action, leading to a life endowed with bliss and free of vice. Further practice leads to the next stage of concentration.

Concentration

In this stage I am able to dive into the pure experience that the thoughts in the second stage have created. The thought 'I am a pure soul' gives an experience of purity; 'I am a child of God' gives an experience of filial love, and so on. Thoughts lead to experience. And from such experience, the moment I start contemplating God, I am able immediately to switch my mind to Him as easily as switching on a light. Very few of my thoughts are now frittered away and, with God as the focus of my thoughts, I simply become lost in this connection.

Realisation and absorption (Samadhi)

Concentration leads to the final stage of realisation in which I am fully absorbed in godly bliss. In this stage, I attain the highest form of spiritual consciousness. I am totally aware of myself as an incorporeal soul and of God as the Supreme Soul. What are God's qualities are my qualities. We are equal.

In this super-consciousness, I experience Shiva Baba as He is. Body-consciousness is lost completely. With the mind focused on God, the fire of *yoga* burns at full blaze, purifying the soul and melting away the alloy of negative *sanskaras*. Past sins are incinerated and the soul regains its original attributes of purity, peace, power, love and bliss. The effort is so intense that I continue to feel divine ecstasy and intoxication long after *yoga* practice is over.

Meditation exercise

Being a lighthouse for the world

Sitting in front of Baba, I experience rays of light and bliss descending on me... and through me into the whole world... I feel these rays charging the atmosphere with vibrations of purity, love and spiritual calm... I am bathing in golden-red light... Strong currents of spiritual might are emanating from me in all directions... I am a spiritual lighthouse... I have the deep realisation of being separate from my body... I feel that I am a brilliant point of light with rays of very high intensity bursting and darting forth from the soul for the service of the whole world… There is no feeling of my body and no conscious thought, except that of being absorbed in the peace and bliss of Shiva Baba's love… I feel completely fulfilled and that I have obtained the ultimate,… the final and highest destination.

Raja Yoga – the essence of all yogas

There are so many systems of *yoga* that it is thought that, for each aspirant, there is a particular brand of *yoga* that is suited to him or her.

Let us examine some of them.

Bhakti Yoga

This is the *yoga* of devotional love. It is for those who, through loving worship, wish to unite themselves with God, a particular deity, prophet, saint or *guru*. Through prayer and the faithful observation of certain rituals, the followers seek to become one with their chosen figurehead. A Raja Yogi is a *Bhakti Yogi* in the sense that his or her love is totally channelled in the direction of the Supreme Father and no corporeal being. But, since the love is a natural one between a child and father, there is no need for rituals or acts of worship. The filial bond is sufficient. Instead of the attitude, 'Our Father, You are the greatest; I am nothing but a miserable sinner…', there is a deep, natural love based on the similarities between the soul and God and not on the differences. For a Raja Yogi, the highest act of devotion is to reflect God's qualities in one's practical life.

Those who try to find spiritual development only through ritualistic devotion will tend to show great development of their emotional side. But wisdom is not based on love alone. Because of the tendency to have faith without understanding, there is a danger of fanaticism and closed-mindedness. A soul's love for God is built on knowing Him as He is.

In this respect, the Raja Yogi bases his love on knowledge of God. No matter how elevated a deity, a prophet, a saint or a human being is, he is not God, God is the one to whom even the prophets and saints turn for succour.

Those who open themselves to love only, without a corresponding development in awareness, may become very sweet and loving but, because of a lack of understanding, circumstances can easily take advantage of them. This is evident in many of the wars that have stained our history; wars fought with a religious zeal because of a fanatical love for someone or some ideal, yet clearly demonstrating a paucity of understanding.

Gyan Yoga

This is the *yoga* of knowledge and is for those who are attempting salvation through the study of the sacred books of wisdom and esotericism. Scriptural scholars and spiritual intellectuals could be considered *Gyani Yogis*. The danger here is developing arrogance and one-sidedness, where there is not the balance with true devotion, or bhakti, for God. Love sweetens our understanding just as knowledge matures and directs our love. Love uncontrolled by knowledge can be like a hose that is turned on but, having no hand to guide it, it whooshes and gushes forth making its proper use impossible.

When the soul has *yoga* with God based on wisdom, it becomes protected from the misuse or abuse of its energy. With the depth of perception that spiritual knowledge brings to the soul, the soul is able to recognise clearly all the obstacles that come on the path, and overcome them. When necessary the soul is able to direct its energy through the 'hose' of the mind, to put out a fire with full force or let out just a few drops to water a flower. Without such control, and without pure love for other souls, we find ourselves, sometimes trying to put out the fires of difficult situations with just a trickle or, on the contrary, turning on the 'tap' at full force. So Raja Yogis see that the balance between love and knowledge is essential. Bhakti develops the sweetness and gyan develops the strength of personality.

Hatha Yoga

This is the *yoga* that uses force and discipline in an attempt to unify the energies of the body with those of the consciousness. Through physical postures and breathing exercises, sometimes quite arduous, *Hatha Yogis* are able to achieve considerable control over the metabolism and attain a remarkable level of physical health. For the Raja Yogi, *Hatha Yoga* is practised on a much more subtle level. A natural discipline and force flows from a deep understanding within the soul. The question of putting the body into certain postures is taken only as far as physical health is concerned. After all, the 84 principal asanas or postures that form the basis of *Hatha Yoga* are, in a sense, symbolic attempts to embody a desired spiritual stage. If the soul is able to achieve that posture mentally, then sitting the body in a certain position to achieve the same is rather superfluous. In fact, with practice, the soul is able to adopt a mental posture, according to whatever situation it finds itself in.

Perhaps the most famous posture of all is the *padmasana* or lotus posture. Raja Yogis put themselves in this posture mentally. Besides, when the soul is fixed in loving union with God, the physical posture is not so important. Just as the roots of the lotus grow in the bed of the pond but the flower is a thing of radiance and beauty, floating on the water untouched by the mud and slush, the Raja Yogis live in the world, but beyond it. Even though their 'roots' are in the muck of society, they maintain a mental posture of detachment and purity. Living in the thick of things, they remain pure observers and a source of beauty and radiance for others.

Working from within, one is able to achieve a self-discipline which is well-balanced with love and knowledge. Those who concentrate solely on *Hatha Yoga* believe that, by first disciplining the body, they will be sufficiently relaxed and controlled to undertake the practice of meditation. To be able easily to enter the state of meditation with the thought, 'I am really a soul, the child of the Supreme Soul', makes the attempt to reach self-realisation by performing physical exercises an unnecessary detour. Raja Yoga can be practised by anyone of any age or physical state because all that is required is the faculty of thought. This is a clear contrast to the approach of Hatha Yoga.

Sanyas Yoga

Those who renounce society and their families and lead a life of solitude and contemplation removed from the normal, worldly ways, are called *Sanyas Yogis*. *Sanyas*, as discussed before, literally means 'renunciation'. In India, it has been traditional for the male, upon reaching the age of 60, to renounce his wife and family and take to the life of *sanyas* in an attempt to meet the Creator, though many nowadays become *sanyasis* much earlier.

For a Raja Yogi, renunciation is important. It is not a physical renunciation but a renunciation of negativity. A Raja Yogi in contrast to *sanyasis*, stays within the family, maintaining social responsibilities, but renouncing all negativity that exists within their physical situations. If there is physical renunciation but the thoughts are still pulled to the being or object that is being renounced, this is artificial. The thoughts of a Raja Yogi are pulled to the Supreme Soul because there is the recognition of the sweetness of that unlimited source. The soul thus has a natural and automatic renunciation of qualities that could impinge upon that sweetness.

A spiritually purified state of mind does not demand renunciation of hearth and home or the performance of fasts and penances, but lives an enlightened life. True renunciation is not based on repression but on realisation.

Karma Yoga

Some think that one only has to perform the normal chores of life in a spirit of dedication to God to be considered a *Karma Yogi*. The Raja Yogi applies the *yogas* of love, knowledge, discipline and renunciation to his or her practical life and thus becomes a *Karma Yogi*. Because of the ease of relationship the soul has with God, it is able to maintain a love-link while performing any action no matter how mundane.

Because the soul expects no fruit of a particular action, it does not fall into the trap that each action sets. For example, I do a favour for someone and expect some return, even just praise or support. If it does not come, I become sad or upset. In this way, actions lay 'traps'. Acting in the consciousness that I am God's instrument, I am planting imperishable seeds that will bear fruit automatically at some time in the future. I need not worry about the results of such actions. In this consciousness actions are not traps but rungs of the ladder of progress.

The benefits of the practice and study of Raja Yoga

God has been described as *Sat-Chit-Anand*: the Truth, the Conscient, the Blissful. Contact and relationship with Him naturally imbue the soul with these qualities, which are intrinsically original qualities of the soul itself.

Truth

With the knowledge that God reveals, the soul is provided with a perfect mirror: 'How far have I come?' 'How far have I still to go?' One's defects become easier and easier to recognise and to uproot. Truth highlights the tiniest specks of dirt and the soul, having confidence in its true identity, starts to clean itself. With truth, the soul becomes the embodiment of virtues.

Consciousness

Knowledge and appreciation of Shiva Baba's role bring a subtlety of perception that allows one to be able to discriminate and act properly in all circumstances, whether it be in the face of praise or defamation, pleasure or pain, success or failure. There is a subtle awareness of living in two dimensions at the same time: as a human being with a variety of roles and responsibilities, and as a soul, a child of God, with an overall responsibility to help the Father in His task of uplifting the world. So, though I may have to be involved in the activities related to work, family and so on,

I never lose sight of my true task of uplifting all those with whom I come into contact. The conscious soul becomes the embodiment of all powers.

Bliss

In bliss are merged light, love, knowledge, peace and power. It could be described as a total joyful awareness that keeps the soul flying above the negative atmosphere of the iron-aged world. Churning over the idea of Baba's being an ocean of bliss keeps the soul easily detached and yet completely loving when coming into contact with anyone. Bliss is a feeling of super sensuous joy which breaks the limitations of 'I'-consciousness (egocentricity) and allows the soul to become the embodiment of service and an inspiration for all. Bliss is the highest gift we receive from Baba.

Silence

The most immediate and useful benefit of meditation is that the internal 'noise level' of confused and jumping thoughts is reduced to a minimum, as the soul fills with the silence of *Om Shanti*. This permits a coherent and cohesive stream of thoughts to flow towards self-fulfilment. The deep silence experienced cures all ills and is able to pull others into a similar state.

The further list of benefits is immense. The divine fire of *yoga* burns out even the deepest-rooted negative tendency, relieving the burden of wrong past actions. When I attune my consciousness to Shiva Baba, it is easy to control and concentrate the mind and be free from useless thoughts, anxieties, tensions and confusions. When I tap the source of power and peace, my own inner strength and willpower become stronger. This, in turn, makes me more efficient and alert.

> *Like moths plunging towards the flame,*
> *We journey to our home again;*
> *Like flowers open to catch the sun,*
> *Our minds are open to see the One.*

The spiritual powers

As the soul sits in silent remembrance of the Supreme Soul, it fills with strength which manifests in spiritual powers.

The power to withdraw

With full awareness that I am an entity different from my body, I can withdraw from the senses whenever I wish and become a point. In the same way that a tortoise retreats into its shell in a moment of danger, or just to rest, I am able to retract myself from any situation and remain protected. Going within at regular intervals enables me to both accumulate and draw on my resource of inner strength.

The power to pack up

With the ability to go within, I learn how to pack up all wasteful thinking in a second, so that there is a lightness and freedom from burdens and worries. Though there may be many responsibilities, I cease to worry about them. At the time of discharging my duties there is full attention, concentration and economy of thought, but at the time of meditation, thoughts or speculation about worldly obligations do not intrude. I have an automatic 'escape valve' of going deep into the self, checking thoughts on a subtle level and experiencing a relationship with God. Preoccupations with limited external activities, past, present or future, are 'packed up' and the soul's unlimited consciousness is revealed.

The power of tolerance

In this light frame of mind, I am able to tolerate all types of situations and people, to the extent that there is no sense at all of having to tolerate something or someone. With the understanding that each one is simply playing his or her role in this immense world drama, impatience, irritation and annoyance disappear like mists before a strong sun. The soul sits under the tree of life enjoying the variety of branches and scenes of existence. There is natural comprehension of all.

The power to accommodate

Just as the ocean accepts all the different rivers that flow into it, whether polluted or clean, I am able to adjust myself to all that is happening around me. Just as a person dresses fit for an occasion, I learn to 'dress' myself with the appropriate knowledge for a person or scene and thereby maximise each opportunity to create benefit. It doesn't mean that I adjust to an atmosphere which could be weak and impure, but that I press the right 'internal buttons' so that any weakness and impurity does not affect me. Not only that, but I am able to change such a scene into one of benefit.

Let us take an example of adjusting oneself to a particular person. The person in front of me is dying of thirst, but I don't know that and try to give him diamonds, gold, anything, except water. All he wants is something simple and will value nothing else. If I don't have the power to adjust myself to another, I will not perceive exactly what he needs, but try to give him what I think is right for him.

The power of judgement

Through this self-adjustment, I can accurately assess any situation with clarity and confidence. In a detached, impartial state of mind I judge my own thoughts, words and actions to see if they are beneficial to the scene in which I find myself. I become the judge of myself, never the judge of others. This is reflected in a balance of love and law: spiritual love for all others and the discipline to keep myself within the boundaries of the highest code of conduct. If I see someone breaching the divine laws, there are two possible attitudes. If he is acting wrongly and doesn't even perceive it, then I can feel mercy and the will to inspire him to correct himself through my own example. If he does perceive it and is making an effort to overcome it, I can feel respect and will him further towards divinisation with my thoughts.

The power of discrimination

With such equilibrium I can discriminate accurately between the real truth and the apparent truth, between things of temporary value and those of eternal value and between the superficial and the subtle. This power helps me recognise the traps that Maya (illusion) puts before me, however sweetly decorated and enticing. It seems that it is Maya's job constantly to test the soul and so falsehood comes disguised as truth many times to examine my level of progress. Only with discrimination power can I see through the disguises and act confidently in the most positive way.

The power to face

Having confidence in one's spiritual state brings the courage to face any type of situation. Believing that I am God's instrument in thought, word and action, allows me not only to confront any scene but to influence it in a positive way. For example, a close member of the family 'dies' (leaves the body). Without tears and with knowledge, I face it to such an extent that my confidence and compassion take away the grief of the other members of the family.

The power to face reality comes when I have conquered all fear and doubt, especially about my abilities. If I know myself, my talents and specialities and have the company of the Supreme Soul, I can take on anything and emerge, having caused benefit.

The power to co-operate
The natural result of all the powers is that I am able to share with others the tasks and qualities that my Father has given me. There is no feeling of competition; so I can give as well as accept suggestions as to how to proceed with the task of uplifting the world. Co-operation allows me to share my virtues and specialities and to learn from the qualities and talents of those I am co-operating with.

The effects of Raja Yoga on physical health

In the spiritually 'demagnetised' condition, the soul is completely at the mercy of the surrounding physical and vibrational phenomena, and its life force flows outward and is dissipated. In the body-conscious condition the aging process and deterioration of the cells are accelerated through the hyperactivity of the senses.

In the spiritually 'magnetised' condition the reverse occurs. By shunning grossness and remaining in the state of *yoga* with God, the body and brain cells are rejuvenated, as if by some spiritual elixir. The sensory tumult is stilled in the midst of all possible temptations. A fathomless peace descends on the mind, which has the remarkable effect of 'cooling' or 'de-exciting' the sense organs so that they don't impede spiritual progress.

The state of the body is a reflection of the state of the soul, not only because of past karmic factors (illness which comes as a result of past negativity), but because of its present state also.

For example, when the emotion of fear passes through the mind, the endocrine system starts pumping adrenalin through the body to prepare it for a surge of energy: to run away in huge strides. It is easy to note the cause-effect relationship between fear and adrenalin. In the same way all of the mental oscillations provoke compensatory secretions throughout the body. Internal rage is accompanied by heavy breathing, fast heart beats, red face and so on. This relationship between body and soul is the reason most physical diseases spring from a psychological origin. It stands to reason that any lessening of harmful secretions through reducing emotional causes will promote sound and lasting health.

Of course there are other factors which give rise to health problems; pollution, unhealthy lifestyle, lack of exercise or wrong diet and so on. Through Raja Yoga and its consequent positive lifestyle and through a pure vegetarian diet *(see Chapter 8),* ill-health can be minimised. The removal of stress and tension has to be one of the most important advantages for a Raja Yogi. Stress plays a huge part in provoking simple problems like headaches and indigestion, chronic problems like asthma and ulcers or long-term illness, such as heart and respiratory problems or even cancer. Health and order in the soul bring health and order in the body.

Important points in Raja Yoga practice

Yoga is not something we do but rather something we have. It is not that we spend 23 hours in an extrovert state and only one hour in introspective self-effort. In this sense, extroversion means to have the attention drawn by all the goings-on outside the soul. True introversion, also, does not mean to sit in a corner and not speak to anyone. It means to pay attention that all thoughts, words and actions are flowing in the right direction. In this respect, the churning over of points of knowledge throughout our active hours strengthens and maintains the yogic state of mind like nothing else.

There are five basic points to churn over. Create your own thought commentaries around each point.

Who am I?

I am a soul. The body is my chariot. All human beings are souls too, my brothers and sisters. I see them with spiritual love. While walking and talking, I see others as souls. Maintaining this vision, I transcend all the barriers of worldly differences.

Whose child am I?

Just as I naturally have the awareness of being the child of my physical father, receiving sustenance and a form of inheritance, so too I can have the natural consciousness of being a child of the Supreme Father. I can reflect on the sustenance and inheritance I receive from Him.

What is my true religion?

No matter how much surrounding turmoil there may be, I can remember that my true religion is peace and purity. I am not a Hindu, a Buddhist or Christian; I am a peaceful soul. Just as people may resist conversion from their religions, I resist any attempt to pull me away from my true religion of peace.

Where and what is my home?

Just as people love their homeland, I can have the same natural love for my original home, the soul world. At the same time I can be aware of my original form of light and power. In this way I can transcend any situation that faces me. I am also aware that I have soon to return home and so I must settle all my karmic accounts.

How is this world a drama?

With the consciousness of the cycle of 84 births, I can see my role and the roles of others in a perfect and unlimited drama. Even though others and I are playing parts, we are separate from the roles. Now that I know the Director and story of the whole drama, there is no point in getting upset over tiny little scenes. I know the beginning, the middle and the end of the drama and so I can bring out again the *sanskaras* that I had in the beginning: those of peace, love, purity and happiness.

Chapter 8 Perfection – the Transformation of the Self

The state of perfection

History is a many-pronged fork pointing to as many different concepts about the perfect state of the self as it does about God.

In classical Hinduism, there is the idea of perfection through the merging of the soul with God, *Brahman*. The soul is supposed to lose its individual identity and leave the cycle of birth and rebirth. The aim is to get away from this world of 'nothing but suffering' and spend the rest of eternity 'merged in the light of God'.

There is also a belief that the soul transmigrates through 8,400,000 species and then ultimately arrives at the Godhead as a 'perfected being'. Some of these perfect beings are believed to take rebirth here voluntarily to help those less fortunate than themselves. There are so many messengers, prophets, saints and sages, supposedly here for the salvation of humanity; yet their teachings are at variance. Each one has a different thing to say and a different way of showing it.

In the Judaeo-Christian philosophy, the idea of perfection has been reduced to the goal of one life and a thereafter of either the bliss of 'heaven' or the damnation of 'hell'. These alternatives are meant to inspire hope or fear as the basis of action. Faith takes the lead. Without an understanding of reincarnation it is impossible to explain, for example, the purpose of a baby who has a life of one day and thereafter eternity in 'heaven' or 'hell'. This contravenes the law of *karma*. How could such an insignificant cause give such an extended effect? In recent Eastern and Western traditions, the possibility of perfection has hardly been mentioned. The majority of beliefs assert that the perfect state only comes after death and that all efforts should be directed towards a good 'after life'.

In contrast to the idea of perfection in 'another region', there is the idea of a perfect life in a perfect society in this physical world. The ancient Egyptians believed in such a perfect paradise – known as the 'Osirian Fields' – where men and women lived as equals. There was harmony and an inexhaustible abundance of fruits and grains: complete prosperity. In order to go there after death, on the day of judgement, each one's heart was weighed against a feather. If the heart was heavier than a feather, the soul was sent to a fiery hell. The legends of all the religions pertaining to 'paradise on earth' are strikingly similar to this Egyptian idea.

So we have basically two ideas about the perfect state:
- A state of perfection in the company of God in some region high above, freed from the flesh
- A state of perfection in an ideal society, in this physical world.

Mukti (liberation) and *Jivan Mukti* (liberation in life)

Each soul has experienced liberation both in the soul world (*mukti*) and in the physical world (*jivan mukti*); the former being liberation from matter, and the latter, the liberation from the soul world into matter. The degree of liberation is relative to each soul's part.

Some souls take a maximum number of births (84) per cycle and consequently spend very little time in the soul world. They have accumulated such spiritual power and such a high level of perfection through their efforts in the confluence age that they play bigger roles. Other souls take the minimum of one birth per cycle and spend the rest of the 5,000-year drama in the soul world. However many births a soul takes, it has the experience of both *mukti* and *jivan mukti,* relative to the role that it has to play. Even a soul who takes only one birth per cycle has an experience of both liberation and bondage.

Most religions, unsurprisingly, lay greater emphasis on the liberation from the flesh in the company of God, and not on liberation here in this world. The reason for this is that the majority of souls began their parts after the end of the silver age and so complete and unlimited liberation in life is not within their experience.

Different souls, different capacities

Every single soul in this drama is eternally different from every other soul. The difference is based on the innate *sanskaras* of each one. It is the latent *sanskaras* which determine the role that we have to play here on this world stage. Some souls have *sanskaras* for 84 births and some have *sanskaras* for one birth, two births, three births and so on. Obviously, since the population was initially small and has been growing exponentially, there are many more souls that have just a few births than there are 84-birth souls. Since *sanskaras* are eternal, the number of births a soul takes is the same every cycle.

Each soul has a capacity to absorb spiritual power according to the role and subsequent number of births it will take. That capacity is eternal. Relatively speaking, some souls have the capacity of a 'thimble', some that of a 'glass' and some that of a 'well'. The 'thimble' soul within the brief span of its births will experience both happiness and sorrow as it passes through its own *sato* (pure), *rajo* (middling) and *tamo* (impure) stages. As it exhausts its spiritual power, the soul begins to search for what it has lost, but the search is governed by its capacity. It will not seek for anything outside the parameters of its own experience. Similarly the 'glass' soul will pass through its *sato, rajo* and *tamo* stages over the span of a greater number of births, and since it has a greater capacity, will search harder to fill itself as it exhausts its stock. The 'well' soul with the greatest number of births, both searches the most and needs most fulfilment.

Yet, when God comes to give His inheritance, He gives equally to all. Since each soul has a different capacity to accept that inheritance, the souls become 'numberwise' in terms of spiritual power. This will determine at what point they descend into the cycle. With God's advent, the 'thimble', 'glass' and 'well' souls are one hundred percent restored and ready to start the next cycle.

Understanding this requires some deep thought, especially to see that souls are not equal but eternally 'numberwise' in terms of spiritual power. It is because souls are 'numberwise' that the chronological sequence of births can be eternally maintained. At the end of each cycle, all souls are 'perfected' for the new cycle. Because the capacities are different, the desires are different. The souls that lived in the golden and silver ages will search for that experience. The souls who have never experienced those ages will never search for that experience nor believe in it.

Perfection in life

Real perfection is achievable on earth. That humanity aspires to be better is actually proof that this perfect state has been previously experienced. The golden and silver ages were dropped from history and exist now only in myths and legends and subconscious feelings. The search for the Holy Grail, the Fountain of Youth, the Golden Fleece or the Nectar or Elixir of Life are allegories of the search for perfection. Real events have merely been perpetuated in the human memory as myths.

Perfection is the aim of human existence. The seeds are sown here and the fruits are received here. Both the perfect and imperfect states exist on earth. A perfect life in perfect surroundings is just as valid as an imperfect life in imperfect surroundings. When heaven exists, there is absolutely no trace of hell and, when hell exists, there is no trace of heaven. The state of perfection in the golden and silver ages is a hard-earned reality.

The perfect code for living

Clearly, human beings are more than just social animals or creatures of habit. The ancestors of humanity were perfect, divine beings and then, through rebirth, became more and more attracted to matter and fell by degrees. Those very souls are alive today, scattered among the world's religions and wondering why the world has become so degraded. Indeed, everyone who has ever been born in this world is still here!

Since the end of the silver age there have been many attempts to regulate the slowly degrading behaviour of human beings. Laws and taboos have become so complicated now but, because the loss of understanding was an inner one, all imposed systems of reform and restriction have had little effect.

If established policies and regulations are based on false premises, then naturally the effect will not be real. For example, nowadays just look at the plethora of legislations, law courts, judges, lawyers, penal codes, prisons and police. At the same time, look how little lawfulness there really is. Certainly everyone is breaking the divine laws of harmony.

In the religious field, movements of voluntary penance, intended to punish the human spirit for its waywardness, could do little to stem the downward flow of the drama.

The self, God, the 'home', the purpose of life, the past, present and future have all been forgotten. In action, what is truly wrong and right has been forgotten. This is why God gives us the perfect code for living. It is that perfect balance of love and law which plants the sapling for the golden-aged society.

The natural way of life

Though we live unnaturally, we strive to find and understand peace and harmony in a natural way. For example, the tranquillity of nature appeals to the vague recollection of the original nature of peace which lies in the subconscious.

Through contact and relationship with God the veneer of falseness built up over many births is stripped away. Though we have bodies of different colour, size, age, sex, we have to look at and understand everyone as souls acting in the drama of life with each other, with other species and with the elements of matter .

The steps required to return to the perfect, natural state
Knowledge
Out of the renewed relationship with the Supreme Father comes a deep awareness of what is beneficial and what is not beneficial, what is spiritual and what is physical. The soul naturally gains a distaste for grossness since it knows that this impedes its relationship with God. Our appreciation of the deep wisdom of Baba leads us to a love of all things. We thus come out of the whirlpool of lust, anger, greed, ego and attachment.

Through the practice and development of *yoga,* the soul is built up by Shiva Baba, who re-creates it by renewing its spiritual strength. It is not a matter of changing the self, it is a matter of returning to one's true self through the link with God. I experience everything directly from the source; so I need nothing. A non-violent restraint of the mind leads to the love-born remembrance of Shiva Baba.

Having an aim and objective
It is the end of the cycle of 84 births and we know the balancing of accounts is drawing near. We know the new age must be one of complete harmony, and it is being established on the basis of the souls becoming pure now. So the souls align themselves to become as royal, pure and elevated as Lakshmi and Narayan. The mind, intellect and *sanskaras* are directed towards that perfection. An aim and objective for one's life ensures the right steps. As far as the aim is clear, the steps and efforts will be full of determination.

Conquest of the senses
Sense-gratification prevents me from working in the region where spirituality is effective. The soul tumbles at the mercy of the senses, sense objects and sense experiences. Even in dreams, the senses and sense objects pervade. Those who are entirely preoccupied with the material world find difficulty in remembering God and developing spiritually. The mind has to be disconnected from the engines of the senses and connected to the powerhouse of spiritual energy, God. The senses draw our mind towards the various flavours, colours, sounds and sensations. When we have satisfied one desire, we buzz like a bee from one flower to another, searching to satisfy another desire. The memory of sensual pleasures takes

us again and again to the objects of desire. Such desires cause many interfering thoughts in meditation.

The mind can only be truly concentrated on God when it is beyond the pull of the senses. Even in the last moments of life, the senses and their objects stand in the way of a quiet departure from the body. From birth to death, the soul labours under the illusion that the senses and their objects are the sources of happiness. It can only reach and realise the Supreme Soul by crossing the minefield of sense attraction and excitement.

In the same way that a rocket shoots beyond the earth's gravity, the soul realises that the beauty of things and people is illusory and is able to fly to the true source of beauty, Shiva Baba. It is the soul that bestows life and beauty to the otherwise inanimate body. One who looks to physical beauty without seeing the spiritual beauty is like one who tries to taste a beautiful fruit which is only made of clay.

Conquest of vices and inculcation of virtues

Through *yoga* with Shiva Baba, the shadows of negativity will naturally be replaced by His virtues. While in action, it is necessary to reinforce the experiences of meditation by avoiding negative and wasteful thoughts and to develop consciously the divine virtues of tolerance, serenity, humility, compassion, sweetness, generosity and clarity.

Leaving negativity and absorbing virtues

Just as darkness is the absence of light, negativity, which manifests as vice, is merely the absence of spiritual light. Through the influence of negativity the sense organs waste away the 'light' of the soul.

The question of vice, or sin, has been of paramount importance to theology. No matter how much legislative or religious control has been imposed, nothing has been able to stem the internal wasting away of the 'light' of the soul.

Light has a source but darkness does not. Darkness is not created by any source but is rather the absence of one. In the same way, the negative forces do not stem from the real nature of the self but are simply symptoms of a lack of spiritual power or light. As spiritual power declines, symptoms of malaise appear as anger, greed, ego, lust, attachment and related vices.

Conversely, as the soul's power increases through *yoga* with the Supreme, the vices automatically disappear. In fact, problems are not fundamentally caused by a particular vice, it is a question of the extent of one's power. If I am weak, the *sanskaras* most related to vices dominate my experience. If I am strong, they do not have a chance to affect me.

The negative forces have often been personified as 'Satan' or 'Maya' but, in fact, there is no such being. The 'devil' describes a level of body-consciousness. There is no one outside whom we can blame. The vices are symptoms of individual ignorance and loss of power, which appeared only when our original creative powers subsided at the end of the silver age. The soul's power fell below the level necessary to control matter and the senses; thus the vices had a ripple effect. Through 63 births of deeper illusions the soul was more and more propelled by them, until today when they appear to be an intrinsic part of our 'real' nature.

How many times do we hear, 'Oh, he's angry like that…', 'It is my nature to be irritable…', 'I can't change…' This shows the extent to which the soul's own light has faded and been replaced by the dark curtain of negativity. Therefore, it is better that we do not try to deal with each vice and defect individually; as the soul fills with power, its overall condition automatically improves.

Another point is that, within the soul, there is a deeply rooted awareness of God and His attributes, however much it may be overlaid by dirt and weakness. As this is brought to the surface of the consciousness, automatically our thoughts and behaviour patterns change. The vices appear then as mere perversions of virtues.

In modern psychology it is held that we must express all our negative emotions for fear of repression. However, the fact is that 'letting it out' leads the soul further into subjugation to that emotion. Remembering that thoughts, decisions and actions are formed on the basis of *sanskaras* which are deepened by repetition, the soul can only cause harm by expressing any defect or vice. On the other hand, the psychological effect of repressing negative emotions can be quite drastic. Repression can lead to severe personality problems, even insanity.

We should not keep the vices bottled up inside us, like prisoners. Prisoners are always plotting to escape. If we change them into our friends they can help us. For example, the energy required to be stubborn is almost the same as that required to be determined, except that one is positive and the other negative. The soul learns to transfer such energy. Anger becomes tolerance. Greed can be transformed into contentment. Lust can be turned into a desire for world benefit. Arrogance, or the respect for false identity, can become self-respect. The more I inculcate Baba's virtues, the closer I feel to Him, but if I allow inner disturbances because of any vice, my high stage is grounded. All the power stored up until that moment will leak away. I must recognise that I really do not like being body-conscious.

As I wish for higher experiences, I choose to live the life of a *yogi* with purity in thought, word and action. Obstructions come within and without, but through my link with God, I am drawing so much power that I remain unaffected. This needs soul-consciousness. So, in discarding the rubbish of the vices I have gathered over many births, I become my original form and maintain it through my closeness to God.

Forms of body-consciousness

Lust

Souls are points of light without gender. Love is natural between them. Seen in this light, lust and frustration are only due to a lack of real love. Transitory sexually enslaved enjoyment is nothing compared to the loss of awareness it entails. We understand that there can be no lust between souls.

I see all others with pure brotherly vision. I love the soul, not the outward shape and form of the soul's body. Lust robs me of physical and spiritual energy and leads me ever more deeply into sense-gratification. Trapped in the world of flesh and bones, I am a slave to colour, form and touch. Through the loss of reason and self-awareness, I fall into attachment.

The curtain descends on my power of discrimination as the intellect is weakened. Lust is a feeling that waxes and wanes. As it waxes, correspondingly, spiritual vision and understanding dims. As it wanes, I come back to my senses. The desire to satisfy the sexual craving is perhaps the most basic of instincts related to body-consciousness. This egocentric desire to satisfy, basically, the sense of touch, robs the soul not only of its reasoning power but also of its self-respect.

When there is the realisation of the power of the soul and of the opportunity to be an instrument for world benefit, sexual desire can be sublimated easily. As the soul is involved in uplifting others, assisting in their spiritual birth, the constant preoccupation with sex and its ramifications that normally assails someone living in the iron age, fades very naturally. Eventually the emotional storms that accompany it cease. In fact, when the sense organs are used in service of others, the karmic reaction is that they are purified.

Attachment or possessiveness

Pure love is spiritual. Its misplaced forms are attachment and lust. Yet people regard attachment as the 'glue' that keeps the household and family unified. In reality, the people or things that I consider as 'mine' end up as my captors, binding me in a net of worries and fears. The people or things that I cling to through attachment are compensations for the insecurity of the soul, so lost in matter. Spiritual love is unconditional, but attached love imposes so many conditions according to the likes and dislikes of the parties involved. Instead of being the thread of happiness and unity as it is supposed to be, it is the cause of grief and anxiety within any relationship.

For example, a child is born and the parents think, 'This is our child. Thank God.' Yet, if the child were to die, they would weep and become lost in a maze of negative thoughts, none of which could bring back the child. In this case, the 'child' is the body which has died, not the soul. The parents are not the creators of the personality, the soul, but only of its 'vehicle'. The soul is the child of God and no human soul has the right to own another through the words 'my' or 'mine'.

In this case, as with lust, we can also see that the basic motivation behind attachment is selfishness. I place importance on a relationship only because I feel there is benefit in it for 'me'. In body-consciousness those benefits are illusory, transitory. A *yogi* clings to the attributes of God and becomes unburdened from the subtle chains of attachment to limited things and beings. He becomes unlimited, unbound. The natural state is one of comprehension and freedom, and no possessiveness or 'my-ness'.

Ego or arrogance

Thinking highly of one's wisdom, wealth, physique, beauty, experience, social status or family creates the delusion, 'I should be loved or respected for these things.' This self-love, or rather, conceit, removes all sense of reality and generates many false notions. On top of that it usually backfires. Searching for respect and regard through a glorified image of myself, I will not find it. This just breeds discourtesies. I think that the whole world revolves around me and should listen to my opinions. Both the superiority complex ('I am the best') and the inferiority complex ('I am no good') are forms of arrogance because the thought process is egocentric and the repeated word 'I, I, I' is predominant. Because of internal confusion of identity, the soul wishes to find security by winning the attention of others.

The natural state is love for one's true self and others. Ego is love for the physical identity and its temporary masks. Even though we suspect we are weak, we seek to prove our strength before others. As *yogis* we redirect this self-love to God and through that love-bond we are able to love all others and maintain our self-respect. We remain unaffected by praise or insult. The soul no longer sees the world relative to itself. It can see others in their own right and naturally respects their opinions. In the egocentric state I am the 'sun' and others are my 'planets' but in the yogic state God becomes my 'sun' and I see all others in relation to Him, rather than in relation to me.

Anger

Anger is the negation of love, which indicates that the angry soul actually needs love. It burns the soul and others in connection with it and disturbs the natural state totally. People mistakenly believe that anger can bring a situation under control, thereby creating a 'satisfactory situation'. But when I am not satisfied with myself, I cannot be satisfied with others nor can I satisfy others.

Anger is a spear that wounds feelings. When I react with anger, all I am really doing is damaging myself as well as the other. When there is preoccupation with selfish desires, plans and motives, the soul lays itself open to anger attacks or its related forms: envy, jealousy, impatience, annoyance, irritability, disgust, backbiting, sullenness, violence, contrariness, sulking. Each time anger is expressed, harmful secretions flow through the metabolism, causing many physical disorders, such as ulcers, heart trouble and psychosomatic problems.

Raja Yogis, with the understanding of the drama, are able to divert the force of anger to tolerance, largely because they are fulfilled and unattached to selfish concerns. They have nothing that can be threatened by the world of illusions. They only have to remember how Shiva Baba sees other souls and situations and immediately they acquire a spirit of forgiveness and tolerance.

Greed

The natural state is one of sharing and self-satisfaction: to have nothing but to have everything. With greed, I build walls of material possessions, within which I run around in circles in the race of self-aggrandisement, accumulating this, acquiring that.

Greed robs the soul of its dignity as it becomes lost in the pleasures of the senses, especially taste and colour. The greedy soul, stripped of its royalty, attempts to substitute inner wealth with material things.

Greed for food, possessions, power or ambition, hinder the development of spirituality in the soul. The greedy soul can never be content. As a *yogi*, I have 'greed' only for the wealth of knowledge and the love of God. I can appreciate beautiful things but I have no desire to own them. True natural love brings calmness but greed is a fire that burns within and agitates the mind to search constantly for things to acquire and accumulate.

Fear

Fear exists only when we are body-conscious. It is the result of attachment to the physical body, identity, possessions or status. If I am fearful, any harm that the body may be subjected to may cause me to lose my sense of distinguishing between truth and illusion. As a *yogi*, I know and understand how the soul is related to this body and to this world. I understand completely that death or loss is nothing but a change of circumstances which can be viewed impartially and with complete security. My life is in God's hands and my actions are according to His directions. I am resolving my karmic account, so I have nothing to fear from the consequences of my past actions. Fear of an unknown future, which is common to most, is replaced by the assurance that everything I am doing in *yoga* is guaranteed to have a positive result for eternity .

Anxiety and worry

In the natural state there are no ripples of gloom. I am perfectly peaceful and content. Nothing disturbs me. In ignorance, I am worried when expectations meet disappointment, when someone to whom I am attached goes away or has an accident. Worry saps the life energy and drains away courage, zeal, reason, memory and happiness. As a *yogi*, the only 'worry' I have is forgetting God and my relationship with Him.

Laziness

When the weight of past sins is heavy, it produces a type of spiritual sluggishness that hampers the effort to change thoughts, words and actions. This laziness on a subtle level deludes the soul into imagining that 'Everything is all right. There are no problems. I'm OK. The soul rejects the impulse to make internal efforts. There's an expression in India that spiritual endeavour 'isn't as easy as going to your aunty's house'. Many desist from practices like meditation, after only a few tries, because laziness pulls the soul towards complacency, which it mistakes for contentment. Laziness, you could say, is one of the main perpetrators of a negative state of mind, robbing zeal and giving birth and sustenance to the other vices. All of the above negative forces surface in the mind at any appropriate situation unless the soul is in the sweet remembrance of the true Mother and Father. When I know myself and God, these vices and their offspring such as sloth, vanity, jealousy, fault-finding and so on, are intruders into the original texture of the soul. In front of me I can see a state of complete freedom and it is a state definitely without these negative forces.

How to leave the influence of body-consciousness

If there is one vice present, others are not far behind. So too, if there is one positive quality, it can take the soul forward to perfection, gradually embracing all other virtues on the way.

By focusing on my virtues and not my defects, they will strengthen. Because the destination in Raja Yoga is high, defects are bound to appear. If, instead of becoming unhappy, I look at my strong points, without ego or body-consciousness, and see them as gifts from God, they will take me far beyond negativity.

The negative approach of trying to tackle the vices is like a little boy, trying to plug up all the holes in the wall of a dyke. Eventually he runs out of fingers and toes to block the holes and is unable to stop the flow. The positive approach is to take God's help. I go beyond the defects that keep appearing, by seeing myself more and more in the mirror of His qualities.

What else but virtue can I give to God? I can only give the love that is in my heart. I am then able to serve the world with honesty. If the soul says, 'It's too difficult to carry on', Shiva Baba will say, 'Who told you to go alone. Just sit in my lap and I will carry you. You are like a child learning to walk, who wants to leave its mother's hand, but falls over. Stay in my lap and I will take care of you.' The soul takes the positive approach and goes on inculcating positive natural qualities. Automatically, the vices are replaced by virtues.

It is sometimes difficult to realise that any problem or disturbance I feel is because of the influence of the vices within the self. No-one or nothing external can really upset me, but I upset myself. By not blaming anyone else, if I am unhappy, I free myself. The more I become free from body-consciousness, the more tolerant and accommodating I become. Because I am no longer intellectually in bondage to my own identity, I no longer categorise others according to physical criteria. I don't try to impress them with my qualities but with the qualities of my highest Father.

Knowledge of God and His acts impresses upon me that I am His heir, the inheritor of His qualities. When I know God and His most beautiful form and abode, I can develop to my maximum potential and thus experience constant happiness.

Positive qualities

Every scene of the drama calls upon positive attitudes such as humility, tolerance, compassion, mercy, sweetness, cheerfulness, contentment, patience and fortitude. These are the shock absorbers in life, ensuring a smooth and easy passage. The world of the golden and silver ages is the world of positivity. I must inculcate that positive approach in this birth. The method of acquiring these qualities is to see and imbibe only the goodness of others. When I know I still lack something myself, will I concentrate on the faults of others and ignore my own?

Since Shiva Baba is the source of all goodness, I learn to drink only from that One. The goodness I see in others was created by Him. I learn not to drink the dirtiness of human flaws and weaknesses but to have love for all and pure vision towards all. By loving God, I feel complete and natural and easy with everyone. I am helping in God's work of re-establishment of the new world.

Introversion

The greatest key to inculcation of divine virtues is introversion. Introversion necessitates speaking only what and when we must, which saves time and energy. Where talk is useful, I take part with enthusiasm and delight. Otherwise, great benefit exists in staying in silent remembrance. Introversion does not only refer to being physically silent but, as much as possible, having attention on one's internal stage and progress. Likewise, extroversion does not only refer to attention-seeking behaviour but, essentially, to having one's attention pulled by people, things and circumstances, thus creating an inner vacuum. The process of *yoga* takes the soul from sense-gratification to blissful awareness. The basis of freedom from vice is the love of the incorporeal, the eternal. No devotion, pilgrimage, occult power or exercises are greater than the purifying effect of love for God, based on knowledge of Him. Without love, spiritual endeavours further bondages; without knowledge they can be dangerous.

In conquering negativity, the following realities must be faced:
- Sensuous living is devoid of true happiness.
- God exists. He is the eternal Father; so I have a right to His inheritance. In order to be worthy of that inheritance, I have to become pure.
- My natural state is peace and purity and my natural 'dharma' is peace and purity. So I must rise above all distinctions based on physical characteristics of sex, colour, creed and so on.
- God alone is my refuge and source of strength and support.

- The world is always changing. Nothing remains the same. So I must accept the great variety and adjust to giving benefit constantly.
- To be free from upset due to adversity, I must recognise that the events in which I participate have been predetermined by my own actions. In other words, whatever happens to me is exactly what I have consciously or unconsciously created.

The four subjects of Raja Yoga

Knowledge
This puts an end to delusion and blind faith and guides the soul to the true path to God. The soul goes beyond the artificiality of religion and cultivates a natural link with God. The knowledge also highlights the aim and object of human life and gives the soul the right perspective on its efforts and duties. Knowledge provides the 'light' by which the soul can see.

Yoga
This provides the power to bring knowledge from a level of intellectual appreciation into practical life. Because *yoga* is based on love and knowledge, there is a natural and easy relationship between the soul and God.

Dharna
This is the assimilation of divine virtues. Knowledge compels the soul to realise its ignorance and love compels it to abandon evil. Where there is this forged link with God, the soul can easily acquire divine virtues.

Service
This refers to the work that Shiva Baba has given us to elevate all souls up to their respective highest stages. By thoughts, words and actions we remind others of their own degrees of closeness or separation from God, and give them an introduction to the Supreme Soul and the inheritance to be received from Him.

The four pillars of Raja Yoga

Sattvic Diet
Sattvic means the 'highest and purest'. The path of Raja Yoga is immediately facilitated if the aspirant is vegetarian. Since the body comprises what we eat, we should take care to eat only what is pure and

produces a positive effect. Everything we ingest has an effect on the metabolism and, in particular, on the brain. The brain is the 'computer' through which the soul expresses and experiences; so there should be great care taken to avoid foods that might have an undesirable effect.

Meat, poultry, fish, eggs, stale food, spicy and pungent foods such as onions and garlic should be avoided. These are a definite hindrance to meditation. To eat the flesh of dead animals especially runs contrary to the principle of non-violence to which the *yogi* adheres.

Another aspect of *sattvic* is the consciousness that one has when preparing and eating food. Just as the body absorbs the physical elements, the soul 'digests' its vibration content, imparted by the person who cooked the food. For this reason a Raja Yogi eats only that food which has been prepared by someone in the loving remembrance of God and who is following the path of purity.

The normal day's schedule includes several short breaks for a few minutes of meditation which are called 'traffic control' – the control of the traffic of the mind! The times are generally: 10.30am, 12 noon, 5.30pm and 7.30pm.

Good company

As I progress towards the natural state of golden-aged perfection, I can take great help from others on the same path. I realise that those who continue to lead artificial lives cannot really help me, but I can help them. I find myself more and more in the company of those who also aspire to purity and self-transformation and less and less in the company of those who do not. Yet I am imbued with a natural sense of service and compassion for those still in body-consciousness.

Regular study and practice of Raja Yoga

The soul begins a daily routine, including the study of God's teachings, which have come to us through the medium of Prajapita Brahma. Even a short meditation followed by a reading of those teachings and backed up by reflection on the main points is of immense help. Study provides the necessary oil with which the lamp of *yoga* can burn. The early morning is the best time to remain in loving remembrance of Shiva Baba, when the mind is fresh after a night's rest and is free from worldly affairs. Even a business person could spare some time in the early hours from 4 am onwards. This early morning meditation clears and refreshes the mind to make it receptive to the study of spiritual knowledge. A change of the sleeping/waking routine may seem daunting but, if the soul wishes to change, it must give priority to spiritual development and the best time for this is the early morning.

An example of a Raja Yogi's daily routine is as follows:

4.00am	Meditation
4.45am	Tea and shower
6.30am	Half an hour meditation
7.00am	Murli class
7:00pm	Half an hour meditation
9.30pm	Analysis of daily progress chart
10.00pm	Sleep

Celibacy

This is essential if one is to experience the heights of Raja Yoga. A soul which aspires to know and realise the self and God must do only those things which elevate it. Yoga is a state of super consciousness. It is like flying an aeroplane. When the soul is body-conscious, especially with sexual excitement, the plane cannot get off the ground, no matter how hard it tries. The more soul-conscious I am, the lighter I feel and then I can fly. When I see others as souls, the idea of sexual indulgence seems completely alien and gross. It is a 'soul-trap'. I need to fly high enough to reach Shiva Baba in the soul world and experience His attributes. In this respect, the nectar of God communion and the negative influence of 'sex-lust' do not mix.

After all, I am making efforts to take birth in the coming golden and silver ages, where there is total purity. In the world of paradise, conception is a matter of pure love and pure desire. I can see the contrast in the iron age where conception so often seems an accidental by-product of repeated sex, in which the children often arrive, if not unwanted, unloved.

The practical reason for celibacy is that the soul's energy is conserved and channelled in more creative and beneficial ways such as in service of others, the conquest of laziness and tiredness and so on. 'Sex-lust' is the greatest enemy of a Raja Yogi as it increases attachment to the body and to others. It is the complete opposite direction for one who is seeking an accurate and meaningful relationship with God.

The practice of celibacy is not merely refraining from lustful practices but is the means of becoming free from all the fetters of body-consciousness. If one reminisces, one can appreciate what vast stores of enthusiasm, faith, gaiety and energy are dissipated in this betrayal of the self's divinity. Most marriages break down because of a lack of realisation of the higher goals of life.

The lotus-like life

With *yoga* practice I begin to feel as a human being should. I live a non-violent life, in thought, word and action. I live in God's lap, beyond the ups and downs of mundane existence, like a lotus growing on a pond, with my roots in the world but a thing of beauty and radiance for all.

It is not necessary to renounce material facilities and conveniences. I need not exile myself to a jungle or monastery. I need not leave my family or work. What I do need to renounce is negativity and its impact on my dealings and relationships. This is not physical renunciation, but mental. It is based entirely on understanding the natural way to live. I jump over all the hurdles that appear before me and enjoy life, as every moment is but a test for my level of understanding and never an insurmountable obstacle. I can do all this while living a life of responsibility. Indeed, Raja Yoga makes the soul feel inspired to take on the greatest, yet lightest responsibility of all: that of serving to uplift other souls.

> You came to me with a world in Your hands,
> Wanted so much that I understand.
> My billowing heart waits to be filled,
> To sail the winds of Your love.
> Whispers of Truth, flowing through me,
> Threading a beautiful tapestry,
> Lost in this moment and lost in Your light,
> I fly on a carpet of hope.
> Ebbing and flowing, the tides of my spirit,
> Calling me to my ancient past,
> Opening doors to the core of my being,
> Taking me to Your heart.

Chapter 9 Advanced Stages of Raja Yoga

Reaching the highest stage in Raja Yoga

Experience and understanding are the two legs of the aspirant who wishes to walk the path of Raja Yoga to its pinnacle. As the soul understands more, it experiences the opening up of newer and wider mental horizons. As a result of heightened experience, the soul develops wisdom on a deeper and subtler level. In fact, experience can be likened to an ocean; the deeper I go, the further it seems, as if it is unlimited, and the deeper I go, the more I am steeped in experience.

The accumulation of many powerful, soaring, subtle and love-filled spiritual experiences over a period of time leads the soul to become an embodiment of achievements. Having achieved all that is spiritually worthwhile, the soul is able to reach the angelic stage, the *karmateet* stage (free from all karmic accounts), the stage of being a world benefactor.

These stages are not so much matters of sitting in meditation and creating a pattern of thoughts as are the earlier stages. They are rather the automatic results of constancy and the practice of inculcation of all aspects. Sitting and thinking, 'I am an angel', 'I am a world benefactor' and so on does not produce a definite and lasting experience in the initial stages.

The pathway to becoming an angel, a soul who can give blessings to others, who can transmit and control spiritual powers and virtues and who can be a benefactor to this world, is quite steep indeed.

But even so, Shiva Baba shows us how to reach that height. We also have the shining example of Brahma in front of us. His every step, his every thought, word and action, his attitude and vision towards others demonstrated that he was surely pioneering the way to the peak of perfection. That he reached that stage in 1969 was no surprise to those who lived and journeyed on the path of Raja Yoga with him. In his last years it was clear that he had become the one hundred percent embodiment of all Shiva Baba's teachings. His natural and constant stage was the embodiment of all the aforementioned stages. As Raja Yogis we too are traversing the same path. As *Brahmins*, those who have taken spiritual birth from the knowledge of Brahma, our goal is the same as his.

Faith

Through maintaining the Raja Yoga principles, the soul really starts to appreciate the benefits and powers gained. This becomes the foundation stone for a growing faith that leads to further and greater inner victories in the many tests that come on the way. There are four types of faith:

Faith in God

As I become enriched with Shiva Baba's spiritual treasures and appreciate the value of each jewel of knowledge, my faith grows that Shiva Baba is really who He says He is. As the Supreme Father, Baba showers me with love and gives me a glimpse of the unlimited inheritance available. As the Supreme Teacher, Baba explains the meaning and purpose of existence and the laws which govern it. As the Supreme Guru or Guide, Baba provides the orientation to liberate me from all bondages and reach the stage of perfection. Discovering each one of these relationships with Baba, I become firm in the faith that it is really the Supreme Being who is revealing all the secrets of the cosmos and giving me the experience of them as well.

Faith in time

Understanding the cycle, I realise that it is only now in this confluence age that I can make efforts based on knowledge. The knowledge that Baba gives is verifiable by experience and so, with each new and deeper experience, I proceed a step closer to my goal. If this is my last birth in this cycle, and God is here, lovingly showing me the way, then each second should be maximised. If this is the age of rising up out of the shackles of ignorance and impurity, let me take the gift of the lift that Baba is offering. It took me 84 births to descend the ladder from the highest stage to the lowest; so let me value this spiritual birth. It is now or never. The efforts I make now in this confluence age will be the efforts that I make every cycle. To get the best result each cycle, therefore, I have to show great determination now.

Faith in the self

Just as, through experience, I discover that Shiva Baba is truly the ocean of all positive qualities, likewise I discover that I am a tiny pinpoint of conscient light that originally was pure. I really feel that my first births were in a golden-aged world of truth and beauty, and now I am becoming that same deity again. I am emerging from a long night of ignorance. I am becoming pure. Such feelings instil self-confidence and I am able to overcome any obstacle that presents itself. While I do not have this faith, the winds of *Maya* (the illusions of body-consciousness) can still extinguish the flame of effort. When I have this faith, the winds and storms only fan the flame brighter.

Faith in others

When I feel self-confident, I express self-satisfaction and contentment. I feel I am doing something truly worthwhile, that I am actually on the path to perfection. When I am satisfied with myself, I also satisfy others. Moreover, nothing that others can do can dissatisfy me or bring me down. I am constantly on the lookout for the positive aspects of others. By fixing my vision on the positivity of others, I am able to help them bring out and develop those aspects. The faith that I have in others revolves around my vision of them. This type of vision, a well-wishing positive outlook, really helps me to create harmony and unity within my family, at work and among my spiritual colleagues also.

Renunciation (Tyag)

'Renunciation' has the connotation of giving up something that feels good but that we know is not good for us. It conjures up images of caves, hermits, monasteries and so on. Actually, physical renunciation is not required. I do not have to renounce the society or family. I have to renounce the vices that influence my role within the society or family. For example, I don't leave my family, but I leave the attachment that has bound me to so many unnecessary obligations and blind observances. I replace the attachment with love and see 'my' family as spiritual brothers and sisters, souls, fellow actors in this world drama, for whom I continue to have responsibility. I see them as children of the same Father.

Rather than leaving something desirable, renunciation grants me something of immense value. In order to reach the shores of the new world, I have to cast off from the wharf of the old by cutting each of the moorings that still hold me there. I do not stand sadly at the stern waving off the old world, but stand at the bow looking with wonder towards the new. Renunciation is the leaving of things and *sanskaras* that are of no further use at this time of spiritual endeavour.

Intense meditation (Tapasya)

Insofar as I have cast off old negative tendencies and habits, accordingly I can be immersed in meditation. The depth to which I go and the level of power I attain are initially determined by my detachment from the things around me and the love that I have for Baba. So, mentally, I cut all the bondages and momentary responsibilities that may be there and fill my heart with love for Baba, while fixing my mind on Him and on, perhaps, aspects of the different stages. When this union remains unbroken and imperturbable it is called *tapasya*. *Tapasya* is fire that burns away the effects of the past and opens up unlimited horizons.

Service of others (Seva)

With renunciation and *tapasya* I can serve others by passing on to them the treasures that Baba is giving me: knowledge, powers and virtues. True charity is giving something of eternal value. Through my thoughts, words and actions, backed by the power of *yoga,* I can inspire others to claim their inheritance. This might happen through a virtuous action or through a correctly placed word, or simply through a well-wishing attitude. By giving God's introduction to others, they too are brought out of the confusion of ignorance, and their happiness, love and peace can grow. This gives the soul such a feeling of its own value that it is projected further towards the goal of perfection.

Surrender – being a trustee

In order to embark on the road of effort, the soul has to have a deep perception of just how degraded it has become. Otherwise, the impetus to carry the soul to complete liberation will not come. Self-deception and illusion prevent the soul from realising to what depth it has fallen. Weakness, sorrow and suffering seem part of the human lot and should be borne. This prison is a tiny cell indeed, completely limited and full of deceit, from which I can fly in meditation

Sitting at my highest stage where Baba takes me, I look back down on the restrained and weak identity I sometimes adopt and I see the way out. A prisoner will have to surrender to the police but, in this case, in order to get out, the prisoner of body-consciousness has to surrender the ego to Baba. The very bars that confine are thoughts of 'I' and 'my', 'I am this' and 'I am that', ' I know best', 'my position is such', 'this is my talent, my ability', and so on. These thoughts limit the soul within very narrow boundaries. When one's level of knowledge, position and talents are surrendered to Baba, those boundaries disappear and the soul is able to serve with powerful thoughts to an unlimited extent. The thoughts are directed towards Baba in this way: 'It is through You that I am this'; 'It is through You that I use this ability or talent to uplift others.'

Surrender to God is on both the physical and the spiritual levels. On the physical level I dedicate time and energy in the work of unlimited charity. My wealth and abilities I also surrender to Him. It is not that God needs money or even my talents for Himself but He exhorts us to use everything we have in trust so that we can leave the ropes of 'my' and 'mine' behind. As a trustee I am still responsible for what I have and I use that in the service of others. By surrendering the feelings of 'my' and 'mine,' I free myself from the worries and headaches that normally accompany responsibilities. What I have and what I am, in a worldly sense, are for this supreme purpose only.

On the spiritual level, surrender is much more subtle. There is the realisation that it was through my own thinking that I descended the ladder. There is the humble recognition that the Supreme Soul knows best as far as my mind, intellect and *sanskaras* are concerned. Such expressons as 'I think', 'My opinion is the best one', 'My idea should be accepted', 'I know what is best for me', yield to recognition of Baba. As with the surrender of 'my' and 'mine', in which responsibility is retained without the accompanying worry, with the surrender of the ego-sense, 'I', individuality is retained but it becomes unlimited. This is because Baba takes over the reins.

If I think, 'I know what I should do now', Baba will allow it. Invariably, the mercury-level of happiness, peace and power comes down and the soul runs back to Baba like the prodigal son. Then Baba says, 'Let me show you how to elevate yourself. Just follow my instructions.' After such fluctuations, 'I' am forced to admit that 'I' don't know how to control myself alone; I surrender mentally and intellectually to Baba. Surrender is not merely an adoption of yogic principles, nor an intellectual appreciation of Baba's teachings, nor a change of apparel. Selfishness and egoism are replaced by love for Baba and with openness and obedience to His directions. Thus, instead of the ego-self sitting on the throne of the heart, Baba comes to sit there.

The perfect stage

Passing through all these steps, the soul gradually becomes the embodiment of the four subjects: knowledge, *yoga*, the inculcation of divine virtues and service. 'Embodiment', of course, describes the practical application, but there are also certain thought patterns and meditative stages that help create this.

The embodiment of knowledge

After much internal churning over the points of knowledge, the mental process begins to adopt these points and apply them to the scenes going on. Everything is seen with the eyes of knowledge so nothing can deceive the soul. This requires that the soul constantly reminds itself of the following points:
- I am a soul.
- I am a child of the Supreme Soul.
- Now is the time to go home to the soul world.
- I am a hero actor in this world drama.

This last point is not arrogant but, if the consciousness is truly this, action will also be extraordinary and divine. The practical result of being the embodiment of these points is that the soul becomes an observer of drama and a knower of the three aspects of time.

The embodiment of yoga

As with knowledge, *yoga* is not only something experienced when all is quiet and I am sitting alone, free from cares and responsibilities; it is a practical stage as well. The best way to experience *yoga* while performing action is to relate to Baba as a companion. He is the true companion of the soul, the one who is absolutely dependable and who never lets you down. Because He is not limited, He can be with you at any time or any place. With Baba's company I feel I can face anything on the field of action. I am not alone. Baba is behind me, giving me inspiration; in front of me, giving me guidance; and beside me, giving friendship. God's role is my role also. The vision that Baba has of the world and other souls is the vision that I have. In His company I am flying, as He protects me from adversity. I experience complete detachment. My companion is the ultimate authority. Knowing and having Him as a friend, I know and have everything. Nothing or no-one else interests or attracts me.

The embodiment of virtues

The automatic result of being an embodiment of knowledge and *yoga* is that the soul becomes an embodiment of virtues. Through knowledge the soul realises what its original attributes are, and through *yoga,* the soul receives the power necessary to bring those attributes into practice. With God as companion, the soul maintains complete self-respect. There is no need to quarrel with anyone, nor have greed, nor attachment and so on, because I realise that whatever are Baba's qualities are mine.

This stage is summed up in three words:

Nirakari – incorporeal
Nirvikari – viceless
Nirankari – egoless

In the consciousness of being incorporeal, I am able to bring forth my original qualities and virtues. As I practice going into this stage and then coming into action, those virtues begin to manifest in my practical life. Like a tree whose branches become laden with many fruits and then hang low, my life becomes a tree with many virtues, bowing low with humility.

Angelic stage

When I have the consciousness that I am incorporeal, even others begin to notice. By remaining in this angelic, soul-conscious stage, others will also feel a sense of lightness and upliftment in my company.

Angels are thought to be mythical creatures who have a human form with wings, who are always in the company of God and help Him in guarding and protecting souls. Actually, angels are human beings who have divine qualities. The wings symbolise the lightness and freedom of such souls. One of the wings of the angel is to be the embodiment of knowledge, the other is to be the embodiment of virtues. With such wings the angel flies constantly in the company of God. Its lightness is because it has no attraction towards anything in the physical world. This freedom comes from having no bondages; all the chains have been broken. The angel is the embodiment of God's powers.

Because I have the absolute and constant support of Shiva Baba, I can be the support and protector of many others. My language is silence. My love for humanity is unbounded and yet I am completely detached, as Baba is, and no power on earth can shake me. I experience that whatever comes through me in thoughts, words or actions has the effect of blessing other souls, as if I am able to perceive immediately what each soul needs. My thoughts, words and actions are all serving.

The embodiment of service – the world benefactor

When such angelic qualities are experienced over a long period of time, the soul can be a world benefactor. The world benefactor stage is truly unlimited. When everything I have and 'am' is serving others spiritually, then I am a world benefactor. My attributes and actions affect the whole of humanity and the entire physical world, just as Baba's attributes have that effect.

Everything: my vision, outlook, attitude, words and deeds are offered freely and impartially; always seeking to guide other souls back to their natural qualities and to the lap of their Father. In this stage, I am truly God's right hand in the work of establishing the new world. My actions are the highest possible. The soul becomes a ruler and truly follows in the footsteps of Prajapita Brahma.

Meditation exercises

The observer stage

I am a soul,… child of the Supreme Soul… I see the vast drama stretched in front of me from my highest vantage point,… my sweet home in the company of sweet Baba… Within that I see my role… I see others also as actors playing roles,… each one eternally individual,… tiny points of light, playing roles through matter… I am a soul with an eternal role… They are also… I can see that every situation is just a combination of roles and movements… No need to worry about anything… Let me just stay in my home with Baba, watching this endless chain of events swirl around me… I am the observer with Baba.

The angelic stage

I am a soul… Baba is my companion… I feel completely free from the corporeal world,… just a tiny soul in a body of light… The ocean of love is breaking in my heart… and I send out rays of light and might,… like a lighthouse radiating Baba's love,… peace,… light,… power… I experience how firmly my consciousness is planted in Baba's heart… Nothing can shake me.

Seeing the three aspects of time

I am here with Baba,… observing the drama… Having freed myself from the limitation of my present role,… I see all of my roles flashing before me,… my stage in the soul world,… my role as deity on this earth,… the decline,… the role of searcher and worshipper,… searching for the very One with whom I am now… the One who had made me a deity,… the search and now the fruit,… now,… my role in helping Baba establish that perfect world again,… my role as an angel helping God protect and uplift my fellow souls who are not so strong. I see the three aspects of time unfolding,… the past, present and future… I am the angel… I am the deity… I am the searcher… I am the one who finds… I am the one who has the role of a hero.

The soul coming into action

I am a soul,... acting on this world stage... I am with my highest and truest companion,... sweet Baba,... who is ever-constant,... walking,... talking,... sitting,... standing,... working with me. He is my companion, helping me,... showing me... I am with the Supreme Authority... Every action is filled with that force: Shiva and shakti (power).

God's company

I am a soul,... a companion of God... His company colours me with virtues... I see others as He sees them... with such compassion and mercy... as if He can accommodate all souls in His heart... I begin to feel so much pure love for others... I radiate His virtues,... His sweetness... I am His instrument.

Chapter 10 The Spiritual Revolution

The visions of Dada Lekh Raj

In 1937 in Hyderabad, Sindh (now Pakistan), the foundation of a unique spiritual institution was laid. The man who was instrumental for it was a well-known jeweller. His name was Lekh Raj but he was lovingly called *Dada* (elder brother) by his friends and colleagues. Born in 1876, in a small village, he was the child of the local headmaster. Yet, from those humble beginnings he rose to become a merchant prince. Through his business acumen and high ethical standards, he rose to prominence as a diamond merchant. He had intimate contact with royalty and great magnates of India. As well as being a millionaire, he commanded great respect for his humility and consideration for others, especially the poor and the exploited. He adhered strongly to spiritual principles and was a well-known philanthropist.

Towards the age of 60 he was strongly drawn to isolated contemplation of the self and God. At this age, according to Hindu tradition, a man retires from worldly affairs and enters a life of renunciation and devotion in order to reconcile himself with God. Uncertain about their future, he and his wife made a visit to the holy city of Benares. It was quite normal for him to begin each day with meditation and a reading of the *Bhagavad Gita* scripture. One day, however, a wonderful and strange thing happened during meditation. He was pulled into a state of trance and was shown a series of divine visions. He had a vision of physical destruction through natural calamities, civil wars and the use of incredibly powerful weapons (later identified as nuclear arms). He was horrified.

A short time hence the horror turned to wonder: he had another vision, this time of the post-destruction world, as it would be at the end of the 20th century. He saw multitudes of souls leaving this world and returning to a region of light beyond the physical universe. From there, he saw souls descending like tiny stars, which, on coming to earth, materialised into divine beings. It was a world of complete peace, happiness and purity in which humans, animals and the elements of nature were all completely devoid of violence. He had no idea how such a world could be established, nor how the present world would be destroyed. Nor did he have any idea how much time would pass for all this to occur.

In another vision he saw an intensely bright, self-luminous orb of light, which cast him into a state of divine ecstasy. Upon emerging, he said, 'Who was He? Such light, such might!' A voice replied: 'You have to make such a world.' He had yet another vision. This time it was of the four-armed Vishnu who was telling him: 'I am you!' He had no idea that he was seeing the perfect state. *Dada* was greatly shaken and transformed by these visions. He consulted his guru, but the guru knew nothing.

Inspired by these visions, he wound up his business and commenced a completely spiritual way of life. He began to hold spiritual meetings in his home, open to people, irrespective of sex, caste or creed. The class consisted of chanting the sacred syllable *Om* and commenting on the deep significance of the *Bhagavad Gita*. Though he had been reading the *Gita* daily, as he read it now, deep new points were emerging, particularly concerning the way life should be led. Great emphasis was placed on purity and, in place of worship, there was emphasis on becoming virtuous. Of those who attended, many had similar visions and experiences. Thus, the small family community began to grow.

Usually in India, such gatherings were restricted to men. Women were not generally allowed to recite the *Gita* or the word *Om*. Women were considered spiritually inferior and had to worship and serve their husbands as if they were God. In some religious scriptures they were even called 'the gateway to hell'. *Dada,* however, rued the plight of women. He had always considered them equals. Hence, many women and girls were attracted to this gathering, where they found the respect denied to them in the outside world.

At this stage, Dada did not know what was happening. The congregation became so large that they had to move to bigger premises. As the popularity of the group grew, so did opposition to them, mainly because of the adherence to chastity. Dada's house was burnt down and there was an assassination attempt. There was also an attempt to get the group officially banned. However, when the authorities investigated, they found the principles and ideals to be exactly what society needed. Nevertheless, opposition burgeoned and eventually Dada and those who were willing and able moved to Karachi. There Dada established an ashram-style community of about 350 men, women and children. They settled deeply into the study of knowledge and the practice of spiritual *yoga*.

Still Dada did not fully understand the wonders that were taking place.

Anyone who sat near him at this time automatically experienced a deep silence and bodilessness. A young girl arrived, who was so mature in her spiritual outlook and motherly disposition, so efficient and virtuous, that Dada placed her in charge. Despite her youth she became known by all as 'Mama'. Even her own mother called her 'Mama'. During this period in Karachi nothing was spared to ensure that every need of the students was attended to. There were songs, games, trance experiences and the practical discussion of spiritual knowledge. Then a wonderful thing took place. Incorporeal God, Shiva, entered the body of a young girl and spoke to Dada: 'Do you know what has been happening?' Dada replied that he didn't. Shiva Baba began an explanation that lasted five hours. He explained who He was, what He was doing and why He was doing it. He explained what Dada's role would be in the establishment of the new world. He gave Dada the name of Prajapita (world father) Brahma. Later, Mama was given the name Jagadamba (world mother) Saraswati. Shiva Baba explained that the means of spiritual upliftment for human souls was now being made available through the study and practice of Raja Yoga. Thus the real ancient *yoga* system of India was being reawakened through the instrument of Brahma. Thereafter, every day Shiva Baba Himself would enter the body of Brahma and impart jewels of divine knowledge. This knowledge has been lovingly called the *Murli* or 'Flute'. As Baba plays this magic flute of knowledge, he wakes up in us all that is noble, true and good. Until 1969 this practice continued.

Brahma, himself affectionately called *Baba* because of his unlimited, fatherly outlook, never once claimed authorship of the profound truths that were uttered through him. He also was Shiva Baba's student and his study and practice of those teachings brought him to the highest stage possible for a human soul. On the 18th of January, 1969, he attained the *karmateet* stage (free from all karmic accounts, ie perfect) and left the corporeal world. His soul flew to the subtle regions where he remains, continuing the work as God's instrument for the creation of the golden-aged world. From 1969 until the present, both Shiva Baba and Brahma Baba have been coming periodically to the corporeal plane to guide us in our final steps. Through the medium of one of the sisters, who has been with Baba since 1937, they continue to reveal the deepest secrets of the universe. The two souls together are lovingly called *BapDada (Bap* – Father; *Dada* – eldest brother) combining the qualities of God, the ocean of love, peace, bliss, knowledge and purity with the *sanskaras* of the most experienced human soul.

Summary of the knowledge

Since the first descent of God into Brahma's body in 1937, the whole world has been passing through the transformation of the old world into the new world order. This confluence period is the bridge between the iron age and the golden age. Now is the only time a human soul can meet God 'face to face'. The place of the incarnation of the Supreme Soul is India, where the golden and silver ages evolve. Brahma, or Adam, is the firstborn in God Shiva's work of creation.

The Supreme Soul is able to demonstrate His teachings by the example of Brahma. Those who follow his practical example are known as *Brahmins*, the 'twice-born'.

God Shiva reveals:
- Who we are
- Who He is
- Where we have come from and where we are going
- That the true religion of the soul is peace and purity
- Why we have come to this world, this *karma* drama

Only when God introduces these five aspects can we enjoy a natural communion with Him. Without them, we cannot be peaceful or happy, but with them, we see reality and act accordingly. The result is purity in the souls and through that, purity of the world.

There is a huge contrast between human philosophy and the revelations of God Himself. The uniqueness, exactitude and logic of these revelations indicate the source as indeed being the Supreme Father, Teacher and Guide of humanity. God comes to establish the new world simply by teaching souls to remember Him as He really is. Souls desire peace, but they do not know that peace is their original birthright from Him. He teaches not only knowledge but the method to experience His qualities directly.

The flute of knowledge

The following is the essence of the knowledge Shiva Baba has revealed through the *Murli*:

I dwell in the uppermost region of space, the soul world. It is far above this corporeal world of human beings and its sun, moon and stars. I am not omnipresent. You are souls and not bodies. As souls you are brothers. I am the Father of all souls. I am not the motivator of human actions, nor do I guide the behaviour of nature. I perform the unique function of granting fruition to those souls who learn and practice the knowledge of Raja Yoga that I come to teach. I have come to liberate all souls. There have been many messengers giving the message of God, but I am the one of whom they spoke. I am the Father of all souls.

The roles of all souls are predetermined and incorporated in this world drama. It is cyclic, systematic and eternal. Everyone plays a different role in the drama; nothing can be added or subtracted. I am the Father, so I provide for you children, and give you love. As your Teacher, I teach you the true history and geography of the world. As your Spiritual Guide, I guide you back home and liberate you from suffering.

Your original and permanent abode is the soul world. Being actors in this world drama, you descend on earth at your respective pre-ordained times and take bodies. A human soul can take a maximum of 84 births in the world cycle of 5,000 years. All souls continue to take rebirth until the end of the cycle. When you first become body-conscious, you come under the influence of lust, anger, ego, greed and attachment and consequently you become impure and experience suffering. Impurities affect your memory and you forget your own selves, your home and your Supreme Father. At the end of the world cycle, I descend to purify and liberate you souls and take you back to your original abode. Since you have come into this cycle, you have to act. So, while you act, remember that you are souls, remain in peace, remember your original home and have communion with Me.

Just as a cycle ago, the time has come for you children to receive your inheritance of perfect peace and purity from Me, your highest Father, for the coming new world. I have come to change human beings into deities. In this, your last body of the cycle, remain pure. Those who learn from Me how to detach the soul from the body and how to fly to the upper regions by means of yoga power, will be able to relinquish their body as easily as a snake casts off its old skin. The time will soon be gone for you to make these efforts. At that time, there will be no mortal teacher, no scripture, no rituals or prayer that will help souls. Only by remembering Me and the eternal home of souls can you be purified.

Today, BapDada, the ocean of love has come to meet His loving children. This spiritual love, godly love is altruistic true love. This love of a true heart enables all you souls to become loving throughout the entire cycle, because this godly love, soul love, eternal love, spiritual love is the foundation of Brahmin life.

Godly love is the love of the heart. Worldly love breaks the heart into many pieces because it has to be distributed. There has to be the responsibility of fulfilling love with innumerable souls. Spiritual love brings together all the broken pieces of the heart and links them to one. Where there is love for the one Father, automatically the soul becomes co-operative with all, because Baba is the seed. By giving water to the seed every leaf automatically receives water and then there is no need to give water to each leaf individually. To be linked in love with the spiritual Father means to have love for all, and this is why the heart is not broken into pieces any more.

This is the new age, and so let each of your thoughts be new, ever- new. Each action should be the newest. This is called new enthusiasm and new courage. Have you created such a determined thought? Have you taken such a determined vow? As the Father is eternal, so too are the achievements from the Father eternal. Through powerful determined thoughts, you can have imperishable achievements. Consider yourself a multimillion times fortunate soul all the time.

Whatever step you take, each step of yours is filled with unlimited earnings. So you are able to earn limitless earnings each day. Consider yourselves the most unlimited, fortunate souls and stay in this immense happiness: How great and elevated is my fortune. Seeing you constantly happy, others will be inspired and this is a very easy method of service. Those who constantly stay intoxicated in service and remembrance remain safe and victorious. The power of remembrance and service will always help you to move forward The important thing you need is to have a balance of remembrance and service. You must have this balance. It is the balance which enables you to receive blessings. The children who have courage always receive help, owing to their courage. For every step you take with courage, you receive help from the Father for 1,000 steps.

Other books and meditation CDs are available through Eternity Ink.
For a catalogue contact:
Eternity Ink
181 First Avenue
Five Dock NSW Australia 2046
Email: info@eternityink.com.au
eternityink.com.au

Eternity Ink is the Australian publisher for the Brahma Kumaris World Spiritual University.
The BKWSU has meditation centres in over 100 countries.
If you wish to find out about the free meditation courses offered by the Brahma Kumaris and a centre location close to you, contact them through the following:
Australia: brahmakumaris.org.au
Worldwide/United Kingdom: brahmakumaris.org

SELECTED TITLES AVAILABLE FROM Eternity Ink:

PRACTICAL MEDITATION
This is a gentle and simple guide to Brahma Kumaris Raja Yoga. It follows the main aspects of the course with explanations and meditation suggestions.

HAPPY HEARTS AND MINDS COOKBOOK by *Sarah Albion*
A wonderful collection of easy recipes, aimed mainly at children, but titled for families so as not to exclude anyone. Delightfully illustrated throughout.

INNER BEAUTY by *Anthea Church*
Virtues may seem unlikely, old-fashioned concepts today. Yet, in these unique descriptions, Anthea Church brings relevance and a new appreciation to such words as 'contentment', 'determination', 'simplicity' and 'tolerance'. This inspiring little book will guide you into the depths of your own experiences to discover your own inner beauty.

THE SOURCE by *Anthea Church*
If you delight in the paradoxes so often thrust upon the path to spiritual awareness, you will welcome the thoughts and imagery presented in Invocations. Anthea Church offers her explorations of relationship with God in meditative prose coloured by everyday experience. A beautiful gift for spiritually inclined people.

ALPHA POINT by *Anthony Strano*
A collection of relationships with God. 'Father' is something we say easily, but here we find God as our companion... our teacher... our beloved. This book offers us the window of a yogi's experience. Through it we can see the possibilities that only exist when there is absolute love. Only God gives absolute and eternal love.

WINGS OF SOUL by *Dadi Janki*
Dadi Janki is one of the great spiritual leaders of our age. In this beautiful book, she explains ways of responding to life that help us end unhappiness and fulfill our highest potential. Dadi shows how, with God's help, every one of us can make a very practical contribution to a better life and a better world.

DISCOVERING SPIRITUALITY by *Anthony Strano*
The journey taken to discover spirituality is the most important journey the human soul can make. It is a journey within. *Discovering Spirituality* is about that journey and how taking it enables us to become more than we ever thought possible.

INNER SPACE by *Anthea Church*
"As for inner space, it feels in those moments as I place my bulging briefcase on the doormat, that it would take nothing short of a bulldozer to create it" Written by a teacher working in the heart of London, 'Inner Space' fully acknowledges the challenge involved in preserving a calm state of mind. Here is an expression of hope.

MAKING VIRTUE REALITY by *Ruth Thompson*
Virtues, the natural power of good within each of us–whoever we are, wherever we are. Every person uses one virtue or another all the time, as naturally as breathing. We enrich life when virtues come into play.

THE VOYAGERS by *Robert Shubow*
A journey of the soul, a journey through time and space–The Voyagers is the story of humanity, from our most elevated and blissful to our most chaotic and desperate. An allegory to restore perspective and hope.

www.ingramcontent.com/pod-product-compliance
Lightning Source LLC
Chambersburg PA
CBHW071928290426
44110CB00013B/1526